You
Lucky
Dog

You *Lucky* Dog

More Than 30 Craft Projects to Unleash Your Pup's Personality

Valerie Van Arsdale Shrader

LARK BOOKS

A Division of Sterling Publishing Co., Inc.
New York / London

EDITOR: **NATHALIE MORNU**

ART DIRECTOR: **KRISTI PFEFFER**

ILLUSTRATOR: **J'AIME ALLENE**

PHOTOGRAPHER: **STEVE MANN**

COVER DESIGNER: **ERIC STEVENS**

Library of Congress Cataloging-in-Publication Data

Shrader, Valerie Van Arsdale.
  You lucky dog : more than 30 craft projects to unleash your pup's personality /
Valerie Van Arsdale Shrader. -- 1st ed.
      p. cm.
  Includes index.
   ISBN 978-1-60059-249-2 (pb-trade pbk. : alk. paper)
  1. Knitting--Patterns. 2. Dogs--Equipment and supplies. 3. Sweaters. I.
Title.
   TT825.S538 2009
   746.43'2--dc22

                                              2008023391

10 9 8 7 6 5 4 3 2 1

First Edition

Published by Lark Books, A Division of
Sterling Publishing Co., Inc.
387 Park Avenue South, New York, NY 10016

© 2009, Lark Books

Distributed in Canada by Sterling Publishing,
c/o Canadian Manda Group, 165 Dufferin Street
Toronto, Ontario, Canada M6K 3H6

Distributed in the United Kingdom by GMC Distribution Services,
Castle Place, 166 High Street, Lewes, East Sussex, England BN7 1XU

Distributed in Australia by Capricorn Link (Australia) Pty Ltd.,
P.O. Box 704, Windsor, NSW 2756 Australia

If you have questions or comments about this book, please contact:
Lark Books
67 Broadway
Asheville, NC 28801
828-253-0467

Manufactured in China

ISBN 13: 978-1-60059-249-2

For information about custom editions, special sales, and premium and
corporate purchases, please contact the Sterling Special Sales Department
at 800-805-5489 or specialsales@sterlingpub.com.

Contents

The Projects

Introduction

Finally!

This is the craft book dogs have been waiting for. It's all about them and what they've been trying to tell us for years—that personality counts. So why not celebrate what makes your dog special?

Question is: Do you live with a Diva, a Good Sport, a Misfit, a Best Friend, a Rocker, or a Social Butterfly? Don't worry if you don't know. Take the quick quiz on page 9 to find out. It will direct you to a section of great projects especially designed for your dog's personality type. Why should this matter? Consider this case study:

Kay (not her real name) adopts a tiny, fluffy, male Pomeranian mix. Despite all appearances, he's a feisty fellow, full of swagger and attitude. Kay calls him Rocky. (Rocky's delighted with the name; if Kay got that right, she's the human for him.)

Kay, a crafty dog lover, wants to make her pooch something to bring him a bit of fun or comfort. She decides on a cute, soft, squeaky toy. Kay crafts it with love and presents it to Rocky with tears of adoration clouding her vision. He sniffs it, smells Kay's scent, and carries it around just to hear her say, "Aww, isn't that cute," before he buries it deep in the sofa.

Meanwhile, Rocky silently screams, I REALLY WANTED A TUG TOY! But he doesn't have one. Instead, he settles for chomping on Kay's sneakers, which she left under the bed—the new expensive ones that happened to be sitting next to the old, cheap ones. "If only I could have read his mind," Kay laments.

Unlike Kay, you don't have to suffer the consequences of second-guessing what your dog wants. From beds to bandannas, toys to T-shirts, and sweaters to safety gear, you'll find something in this book to please your pooch. Imagine your Diva in a divine Mink Stole Shrug (page 44). Good Sports will look trim and rested lying on a Sporty Sleeping Bag (page 78) after a long hike. The Tug for Two (page 113) is sure to be a hit for Social Butterfly play dates. What Rocker wouldn't want to strut around in a faux-leather Reversible Flight Jacket (page 59)? The Reflective Safety Gear Set (page 28) keeps Best Friends safe during twilight walks. Misfits will appreciate the special Time-Out Crate Cover (page 87) to hang out in and take a break from too much mischief.

Whether a project is sewn, crocheted, or knitted, you'll find all the information you need to make the projects in the basics section. Don't worry about your skill level. The designers—dog lovers all—have created projects that are easy and fun to make, so you can spend more time playing with your pal. Now forget all that stuff about letting a sleeping dog lie. It's time to go make the gear and goodies your dog truly wants. The paws-ibilities are endless!

Basic Dogma

Hey! Hey! Over here.

Yeah, that's it. Here. It's me. You know, *me*, your dog. Li'l Bits, Pookie, Wiggles, whatever you're calling me these days. Think I care about names? Do I? Do I? Naw. All I care about is food. Hey, just kidding. You know I love you—and food, too. Ahh. Treats, bones, biscuits...Where was I?

Okay, so it's a great time to be a dog. I'd even say we finally got our day. Look at all the TV shows, books, movies, and magazines telling you guys what we've been trying to tell you all along—let me bark it out for you—*we're dogs*, each with our own way of doing things that makes us *us*. You call it personality. Around the dog park, we call it instinct.

Why, we can size up a fellow pooch in the time it takes to wag a tail. Doesn't matter how big or little, fat or thin, boy or girl, we have our types down. You've got the **Best Friend** and the **Good Sport**. No mystery there; one's way too devoted for me, and the other, well, it's all about that crazy go-go-go energy. The **Diva** is easy to figure out; just get outta the way, mister. **Social Butterflies** are masters of the meet and greet, if you know what I mean. And **Rockers**, well, they really know how to have a good time. Me, I'm a **Misfit**, all spunk and sass rolled up in charm—and do I know how to roll!

Now, we know you love us sooo much you want to make stuff for us, but sometimes you just get it all wrong. No matter how much a Rocker appreciates the tutu you made for her with the very hands that feed her, she really has her eye on that anarchist T-shirt. And while a Best Friend wouldn't want to be caught playing dead in a faux mink shrug, the Diva is all over it. (Meanwhile, Best Friend is secretly pining for the saddlebags so he can do the heavy lifting for you.) As for me, that crazy-eyed Misfit toy drives me wild, but the Good Sport's crocheted squeaky treat leaves me cold.

That's why this book is the best. There's a section of projects for each of our personality types so you don't have to spend time figuring it out. Of course, that means you'll have more time to spend with us at the park, or hiking, or snuggled on the sofa. Mmm, belly scratches.

You'll find all kinds of toys for fun, fun, fun. Then there are things to wear and lovely beds for curling up on when you tell us to go back to our place. Collars and leashes will keep us stylish and safe. You won't find food, though—but please don't let that stop you. Besides, I already know where you stash the treats. Think about it. Have I ever missed making an appearance when you open the refrigerator door? No wonder my nose is cold.

Pooch-onality Quiz

Your dog knows everything about you. Now it's time to see if you know your pooch as well as you think you do. Circle the answers to the questions below, then add up the numbers to find out if your dog is a Best Friend, a Misfit, a Social Butterfly, a Good Sport, a Rocker, or a Diva. The answer will lead you to the great projects your dog has been longing for.

When you're out exploring urban trails, your dog...
1. trots loose-leash by your side.
2. scents whatever, wherever.
3. holds its head high with tail wagging.
4. spots one tree and hopes for more.
5. checks out the dogs walking their people.
6. walks as if parting water.

In nature, your dog...
1. stays close by.
2. catches a scent and takes off.
3. adores every squirrel, bird, bee, and insect.
4. blazes the trail.
5. keeps looking around for a sidewalk.
6. can't believe you brought him or her to such a place.

At a picnic, your dog...
1. knows where you are every minute.
2. has one eye on the hot dogs, the other on the burgers.
3. works the place like a dance floor.
4. keeps hoping someone will break out the Frisbee.
5. stays asleep from too much partying the night before.
6. finds the best blanket, settles on it, and waits for the adoring crowds.

At home, your dog...
1. wags its tail when you do anything.
2. stares longingly out the door or window.
3. is hoping someone will drop by to visit.
4. sits at the door, leash in mouth.
5. wakes up at noon, same as you.
6. directs every scene.

When you go to the dog park, your dog...
1. plays, checks in with you, plays, checks in, sits with you.
2. shoots out of the gate, headed straight for the action.
3. knows which end is up—greets people first, then other dogs.
4. plays 'til he or she drops.
5. finds the cool dogs and chills with them.
6. walks around the edge of the fence, feigning invisibility.

You just got home from work, and your dog...
1. comes home with you.
2. hides under the bed, hoping you won't notice the sofa.
3. sniffs you all over, reading where you've been.
4. lets you sit down, then brings you the ball, the tug toy, the leash.
5. wonders what's for breakfast.
6. didn't realize you were gone.

For answers see page 10.

Okay, now that you know what I've been whining about, get to work. This chapter will tell you what you need to know about sewing, knitting, and crochet to make all the great stuff your pooch is waiting for. Oh, and if you don't know your dog's personality type, take the quiz above, it'll put you on the scent for tracking down the right projects. As for me, I'm heading for that sunny spot on the rug and a nice long nap. Call me when dinner's ready.

Sewing Basics

Most of the projects in this book are sewn. Straight stitch, zigzag, hand stitching, embroidery; it doesn't get any harder than these easy techniques. Whether you're a novice or an experienced sewer, looking over this information about the basic sewing materials, tools, and techniques used in this book will help get you started.

MATERIALS

You can find all the materials and notions you need at a fabric store. If you can't find the hardware locally, try looking for it on the Internet.

Fabric

Choosing fabric for your dog is easy when you remember three words: washable, durable, and safe. Being able to throw a toy, article of clothing, or dog bed in the washer and dryer is a definite plus.

Look for canvas, twill, denim, felted wool, and fleece. Upholstery fabric that you can easily spot treat is great, too. To protect your pooch, avoid fabric that frays or tears easily, especially when making toys. Rip-stop nylon is tough—great for dogs who tug, trek, and like a toothsome toy. It's lightweight, waterproof, and dries quickly, making it the perfect outdoor fabric.

If your project calls for a smaller cut of lightweight fabric, try using fat quarters. These precut prints

How many points did your pooch get?

6–10 Your pup's a **Best Friend**. The projects on pages 21–33 will make him happy.

11–16 You have a **Misfit**. The projects on pages 83–98 suit this personality best.

17–22 You own a **Social Butterfly**. The projects on pages 99–119 best match this personality.

23–28 Your dog's a **Good Sport** and will love the projects on pages 66–82.

29–34 You've got a **Rocker**. The projects on pages 53–65 are most compatible with this persona.

35–40 Your **Diva** will feel properly pampered by the projects on pages 38–52.

and solids in 100% cotton, cotton blends, and synthetics measure 18 x 22 inches (46 x 56.5 cm), and can be found at most craft and sewing stores.

Felting

Felted fabric is tough—perfect for a fetch toy or tug. Start with a fabric or sweater made of 100% wool. Throw it in the washing machine, set the controls for hot water and a small load, add a half-capful of detergent, and then simply walk away. Machine drying will speed up the process.

This is a perfect way to recycle old sweaters, by the way.

Reflective Material

Webbing woven with reflective thread and reflective adhesive tapes will let your dog be safe and seen at night. Look for the Good Sport reflective Safety Vest on page 67—it turns a human's safety vest into clothing for your friend that will light up his life. Look for reflective webbing at your fabric or craft store. If you can't find it locally, you can find it online.

Hardware

These are the pieces that hold it all together. Side-release buckles, wide-mouth glides, swiveling snap hooks, D-rings, and split rings allow you to clip, adjust, and attach. You can find these at craft or sewing stores or online. You can also recycle them from old collars and leashes.

The side-release buckle is the mainstay of every collar or strap. You can easily thread nylon webbing (see below) through it—the female side has a loop, and the male side has a glide that allows for adjustment. Wide-mouth glides offer another way to adjust and secure the length.

Swiveling snap hooks prevent leashes and straps from getting twisted when you clip them to a D-ring. And split rings let you attach tags—and maybe a charm or two.

Don't forget you can use magnets as fasteners, too. Heavyweight magnets used by hobbyists are stronger than most magnets you can find in sewing and craft stores. Look for them in hobby shops or online.

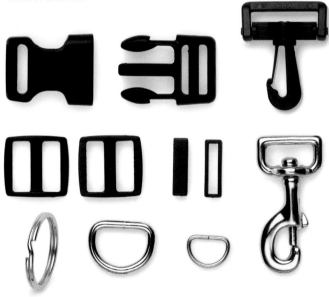

Left to right, top: the female and male parts of a side-release buckle, a plastic swiveling snap hook

Center: glides, a metal swiveling snap hook

Bottom: a split ring, two sizes of D-rings

Right. Simply slide the webbing through the loop in the female part of a side-release buckle.

Below. To thread the male part and glide of a side-release buckle, just do as shown.

Nylon Webbing

Leashes, collars, and straps are made of lengths of nylon webbing. It's tough, water repellent, and comes in a variety of widths to accommodate petite to extra-large dogs. Black is the multipurpose color, and makes a great base when decorating with fabric or reflective material. But don't forget, Divas favor pink! You can find nylon webbing at craft or fabric shops as well as online.

Foam

Choose the thickness you need and cut it to size, or have the foam cut for you where you buy it.

Fusible Web

What would we do without it? The heat-activated adhesive in the fibers provides the magic sticky for fabric-to-fabric applications without any sewing.

Polyester Fiberfill

This washable stuffing makes toys come alive and provides a sweet cushion when making a bed.

Squeakers

All dogs love squeakers—they put the fun in toys! Look for them at pet stores or online.

Puny Pooch

It probably comes as no surprise that the smallest dog breed is the Chihuahua. The breed is classified as a natural toy—which means the dogs inherently started little, rather than being bred over generations to become small. Honors for the world's tiniest Chihuahua may soon go to a Florida pooch who weighs 18 ounces and is 4 inches (10.2 cm) tall. Verification is pending that would wrest the title from a Slovakian dog who measures a towering 5 1/2 inches (14 cm) in height.

I Need a Tug

Tug is a dog game that humans can play too. It mimics the joyous jostling over food that your dog's ancestors enjoyed. The only rule you need to know to prevent your dog from becoming too possessive is that you, as the alpha dog in your pack, control the play and the toy.

Structure the play so you win approximately 90% of the time, making sure your tug-buddy gets some of the glory. It's easy to get carried away, but never lift your dog by its teeth when they're latched onto the toy.

When playtime is over, take the toy and tuck it away for another day. And if you think your dog is aggressive, this may not be the game for him or her—in this case, it's better to play hugs than tugs.

Craft Paper

This is the perfect paper for making small patterns. Many projects have templates you can copy to custom fit your dog.

Embroidery Floss

Floss is essential for embroidered embellishments.

TOOLS

A quick tour of your workspace should yield most of the tools you need.

Basic Sewing Kit

Raid your sewing kit to find indispensable supplies such as needles and thread, scissors, a tape measure, tailor's chalk or a fabric marking pen, pins, and any of the other odds and ends every sewer has on hand.

Sewing Machine

Most of the sewing projects can be made using a straight stitch, but if your machine also has a zigzag stitch, you can use it to quickly stitch over edges and seams to prevent fabric from fraying.

Embroidery Hoop

If you're embellishing fabric with embroidery, using a hoop to keep the fabric taut will make your work easier and ensure your stitches are even.

Transfer Paper or Pens

Use these to transfer designs for embroidery onto your fabric.

The wheel of a rotary punch can make holes in various sizes.

Grommet-Setting Tool and/or Rivet-Setting Tool

These tools will attach grommets or decorative rivets to a collar or clothing. To prevent a curious canine from prying the embellishments loose, follow the manufacturer's instructions to make sure they're secure.

Hole Punch

Use this tool to punch through webbing, fabric, or leather. A rotary punch, used for leatherwork, makes holes in six different sizes.

Above: Tools for setting grommets

Left: A rhinestone-setting machine and its components

Measuring Your Dog

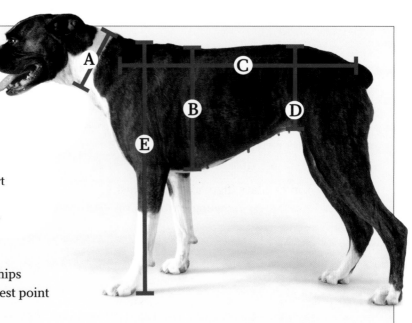

Follow the figure at right to find the essential measurements needed when making collars and clothing for your dog.

A: Neck, measure around where the collar usually sits

B: Girth, measure around the widest part of the chest behind the front legs

C: Length, measure from the base of the neck to the base—not the tip!—of the tail

D: Width (waist), measure around the narrowest part of the dog in front of its hips

E: Height (optional), measure from highest point of the shoulders

TECHNIQUES

This review of the basic sewing techniques and stitches used in the book will get you working in no time.

Clipping and Notching Curves and Corners

Clipping and notching curves ensures the fabric will lie smooth around the curve when you turn the piece right side out. You clip inward curves and notch outward curves after sewing. To clip, use scissors to cut into the seam allowance at several places around the curve (figure 1). Clip close to the stitch line, but be careful to not cut into the stitching. To notch, cut small v-shaped wedges from the seam allowance. As for clipping, be careful to avoid cutting into the stitching when notching. Clipping corners ensures crisp, sharp corners when you turn the fabric. After sewing, cut across the corner, as shown in figure 2.

Finishing Ends and Seams

Dogs are tough on toys and equipment—Good Sports, especially—and an unfinished end or raw edge can unravel before your eyes. To prevent this from happening, take the time to turn all raw edges under, whenever possible, before stitching an end or hem. You can also use a zigzag stitch to overcast any raw edges and seams.

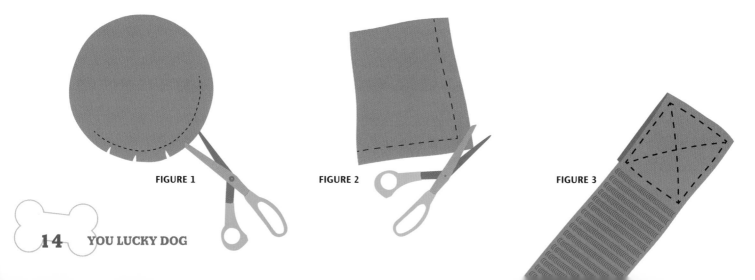

FIGURE 1

FIGURE 2

FIGURE 3

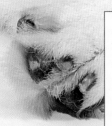

Sewing an X in a square (figure 3) when finishing ends is a durable solution when making a leash or collar—perfect when you have a Social Butterfly intent on pulling to see who's who. If you're working with nylon webbing or cord, you can use a lighter to singe the ends. This melts the plastic fibers together. Be sure to work in a well-ventilated room if you choose to do this—and watch your fingers.

Mitered Corners

Mitering creates neat corners. Miter to shape the corners on a three-dimensional piece, as when upholstering, or to make a clean finish at a corner when sewing a flat trim, such as nylon webbing, to fabric.

Shaped Corner

On the wrong side of the fabric, pin the corner on the diagonal, then stitch (figure 4).

Trim the excess fabric (figure 5) before turning right side out (figure 6).

Mitering a Trim

Fold the trim straight back on itself (figure 7). Then fold the trim down to create a diagonal fold at the corner (figure 8).

Hand crease or press the fold to mark the diagonal. Lift the trim and stitch on the diagonal line, trimming the excess as shown (figure 9). Fold the trim back, and continue stitching the trim to the fabric (figure 10).

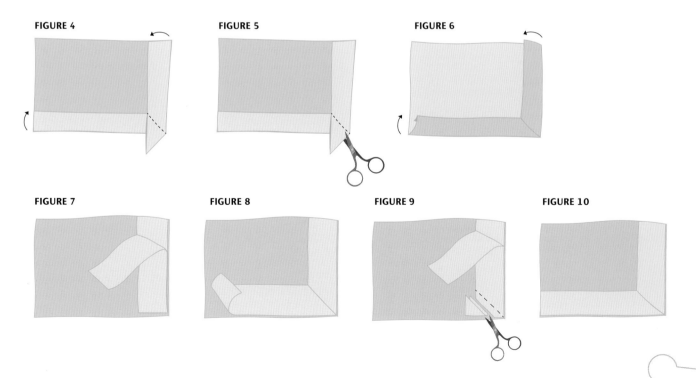

FIGURE 4 FIGURE 5 FIGURE 6

FIGURE 7 FIGURE 8 FIGURE 9 FIGURE 10

Hand Stitches

Hand stitching can add a decorative touch to an edge or hem, or be used when a project calls for embroidery.

Backstitch

Strong and durable, this stitch is great for stuffed projects because it holds up under pressure (figure 11).

Blanket Stitch

Use the blanket stitch when sewing layers together or for finishing an edge (figure 12).

Whipstitch

Use the whipstitch to sew two edges together (figure 13).

Satin Stitch

Fill in an outline with parallel rows of straight stitches (figure 14).

Stem Stitch

Use this stitch to outline a shape (figure 15).

Straight Stitch

Stitched in rows or around curves, the straight stitch creates motifs (figure 16).

Split Stitch

Similar to the stem stitch, the needle splits the embroidery floss when it emerges from the fabric (figure 17).

French Knots

Add playful texture with French knots (figure 18).

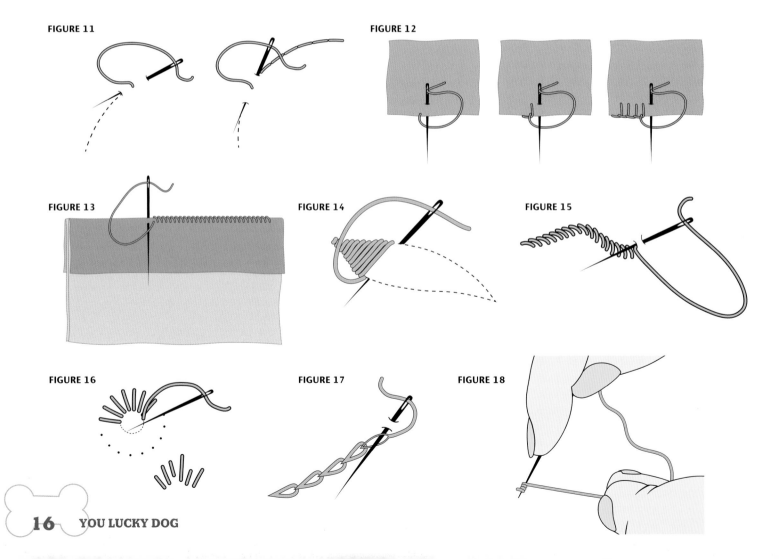

FIGURE 11

FIGURE 12

FIGURE 13

FIGURE 14

FIGURE 15

FIGURE 16

FIGURE 17

FIGURE 18

Knitting Basics

Knit. Purl. That's it! Master these two stitches, and you have it almost made. The knit wearables in this book will make your sweetie the envy of doggie day care—and you'll have pride in saying "I made it myself!"

This section describes the materials and tools you'll need for the projects in these pages, but if you don't already know how to knit, you'll need to ask a friend (not a furry one, though) to show you how, or get a book that explains it.

MATERIALS AND TOOLS
You may already have yarn and needles you can use. If not, here's a good excuse to hit the yarn shop (as if you need an excuse).

Yarn
Since the knit projects in this book are fashion show-stoppers—Divas and Social Butterflies take note—you don't need to be too concerned about day-to-day durability, as you would if making a bed or toy. Be sure the yarns are washable, though, and have enough stretch to easily fit over your dog's head and neck.

Elastic Thread
As the name implies, this thread will add a bit of stretch to your piece while helping it retain its shape. You knit it as one with your main yarn.

Knitting Needle Size Chart

METRIC (MM)	US	UK/CANADIAN
2.0	0	14
2.25	1	13
2.75	2	12
3.0		11
3.25	3	10
3.5	4	
3.75	5	9
4.0	6	8
4.5	7	7
5.0	8	6
5.5	9	5
6.0	10	4
6.5	10 1/2	3
7.0		2
7.5		1
8.0	11	0
9.0	13	00
10.0	15	000
12.0	17	
16.0	19	
19.0	35	
25.0	50	

Knitting Needles
Depending on the project, you'll use straight, double-pointed, and/or circular needles. Use the size specified in each project to achieve the gauge. The chart above is a handy reference when selecting needles.

YARN WEIGHT SYMBOL & CATEGORY NAMES	lace	super fine	fine	light	 medium	5 bulky	6 super bulky
TYPE OF YARNS IN CATEGORY	Fingering, 10-count crochet thread	Sock, Fingering, Baby	Sport, Baby	DK, Light Worsted	Worsted, Afghan, Aran	Chunky, Craft, Rug	Bulky, Roving

Source: Craft Yarn Council of America's www.YarnStandards.com

Stitch Markers and Holders

Markers are colorful circles that help you keep track of your stitches when working in the round. Holders prevent stitches from unraveling whenever you need to slip them off the needle.

STITCHES

Take time to read the pattern before you begin. Each project uses abbreviations for the techniques and stitches used. Refer to the chart below for easy review. Once you cast on, it's knit or purl all the way.

Knitting Abbreviations

ABBREVIATION	DESCRIPTION
( )	alternate measurements or stitch counts
* repeat from *	as many times as indicated
BO	bind off
CO	cast on
dec	decrease
inc	increase
k	knit
p	purl
RS	right side
St(s)	stitch(es)
St st	Stockinette stitch
WS	wrong side

Gauge

The instructions provide the gauge for each project. This tells you the number of stitches across and in rows to ensure your finished piece will not be too large or small. Take time to knit a sample swatch to see how you measure up. Use a needle gauge to check your stitches. If you've never used a gauge, the instructions for use are printed right on it.

Forget Fido

Fido, which means "I am faithful" in Latin, is the all-time greatest dog's name. However, the moniker is as dead as its language of origin when it comes to popularity. The American Society for the Prevention of Cruelty to Animals (ASPCA) surveys veterinarians to find out the most popular pet names.

1. Max
2. Sam
3. Lady
4. Bear
5. Smokey
6. Shadow
7. Kitty
8. Molly
9. Buddy
10. Brandy

If you're looking for a Misfit name, Bandit is listed as number 17, and Princess, the prototypical Diva name, holds the number 22 slot. Tigger, the perfect name for a bouncy Social Butterfly, is number 28. And, Rocky—AKA the Rocker—is listed as 26.

Popularity Contest

Each year the American Kennel Club posts its top-10 list for most popular dogs in the U.S. It's always big news when a breed drops off the list or gets on. (Recently, the bulldog made the cut for the first time in 75 years.) If you love a mutt, it undoubtedly holds first place in your heart, but be aware they never make the list.

1. Labrador retriever
2. Yorkshire terrier
3. German shepherd
4. Golden retriever
5. Beagle
6. Boxer
7. Dachshund
8. Poodle
9. Shih Tzu
10. Bulldog

Crochet Basics

Crochet is very portable, so why not take it along when you're supervising a play date at the dog park? Just a few of the projects in this book are crocheted. They use single and double crochet in a variety of ways—perfect for beginners who want to crochet something comfortable, cozy, or crazy for their canine. The materials and tools you'll need for these projects are described below, but you're barking up the wrong tree if you don't already know how to crochet—this book doesn't provide instructions. However, it takes just a few moments to learn from a friend or a book.

MATERIALS AND TOOLS

It's as simple as yarn and hooks. If you've crocheted before, you might have all you need. Some of the projects are a great way to use up the leftover yarns in your stash.

Yarn

When making a bed, toy, or clothing for your dog, look for washable yarns. Cotton and synthetics are durable, but if you want a softer fiber that provides warmth, go for the wool—or even mohair or cashmere if your pet is particularly pampered.

Crochet Hooks

You would think a hook is a hook is a hook, but a wide selection of styles is now available. Select a hook that matches your comfort level—you'll know it when you feel it.

Use the sizes specified in each project for the best results. The chart above will help you navigate through the different numbering systems. The metric system has become the standard, and is included in the size of each hook.

Crochet Hook Sizes

US SIZE	METRIC
B-1	2.25 mm
C-2	2.75 mm
D-3	3.25 mm
E-4	3.50 mm
F-5	3.75 mm
G-6	4.00 mm
7	4.50 mm
H-8	5.00 mm
I-9	5.50 mm
J-10	6.00 mm
K-10 1/2	6.50 mm
L-11	8.00 mm
M/N-13	9.00 mm
N/P-15	10.00 mm

Crochet Abbreviations

If you're a novice, don't let these intimidate you. The abbreviations are very logical—you'll be speaking the language in no time!

Do take time to read the pattern through before you begin. You'll see abbreviations for techniques and stitches. The chart below includes the abbreviations used in the projects.

Crochet Abbreviations

ABBREVIATION	DESCRIPTION
( )	repeat the instructions inside the parentheses the specified number of times
* repeat from *	as many times as indicated
BLO	back loop only
dc	double crochet
FLO	front loop only
hdc	half double crochet
hdcdec	half double crochet decrease
hdinc	half double crochet increase
MC	main color
RS	right side
rep	repeat
rnd	round
sc	single crochet
scdec	single crochet decrease
scinc	single crochet increase
sk	skip
sl st	slip stitch
WS	wrong side
YO	yarn over

LET'S GO!

Congratulations! You have all the information you need to make the projects in the book. In dog terms, think of it as having passed basic manners in obedience class before moving on to agility training. Here are a few tips that can help:

* It's very important to keep in mind that you may need extra material for your project depending on the size of your dog. When in doubt, measure your dog and adjust the materials as needed for best results.

* At the end of the projects, look for any safety tip that will help you and your pup stay happy and healthy when playing with a new toy or when wearing a fashion accessory.

* Many projects have templates that will help you make your project. The templates can be found in a special section beginning on page 120.

Okay! It's time to pick a project for your pup's type and get to work. If you need an extra incentive, remember, treats work wonders.

The Best Friend

This loyal dog is with you through rain, hail, sleet, snow, and waits patiently for your return home from work every day. She'd rather be with you than anybody else!

Projects

Li'l Buddy T-Shirt. Reconstitute an old shirt into a new fashion statement for your pup. *Page 22*

My Pillow Bed. Your dog will love the coziness of a bed made from your old pillow and will appreciate that it has your scent. *Page 25*

Reflective Safety Gear Set. This gear will keep you and your friend safe during any outdoor nighttime adventure. *Page 28*

Road Trip Booster Seat. Little dogs can now *see* the open road from their comfy bumper seat. *Page 31*

In the Saddle. With this backpack on, your best buddy can carry snacks, water, and toys on outings. *Page 35*

"Hello, comfort."

Designer: **Laura Bersson**

Li'l Buddy
T-Shirt

GO FETCH!

Tape measure
T-shirt
Tailor's chalk or fabric pen
Pins
Sewing machine with a
    ballpoint needle
Thread
Ribbon, in desired width

Finished size: 16 x 18 inches (41 x 46 cm)

Note: *Choose a T-shirt closest to your dog's size. The tiniest dogs may need an infant- or child-sized shirt.*

SIT. MAKE IT!

1. Measure your dog (page 14) to get these measurements: (A) neck, or width of head, whichever is larger, (B) girth, (C) waist, and (D) length. Add approximately 1 inch (2.5 cm) to the neck, girth, and waist measurements for ease of fit.

2. Decide which side of the T-shirt—front or back—you want seen on your dog's back. Turn the T-shirt inside out, and lay it with the side you want to highlight facing up. Fold the shirt over with one sleeve on top and the other lined up beneath it.

3. Following figure 1, start at the back of the collar, measure along the length of the fold, and mark the measurement for the dog's length (D) across the shirt.

4. From the front fold on the collar, measure half the measurement for the dog's neck (A), and mark.

5. Measure down approximately ¹/₂ to 1 inch (1.5 to 2.5 cm) from the top fold on the sleeve. At this point, and starting on the front fold of the shirt, measure across the shirt toward the back fold to mark a point at half of the measurement for the dog's girth (B).

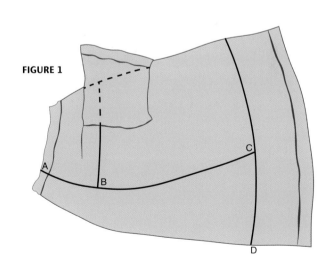

FIGURE 1

6. On the length (D), measure from the front fold and mark a point that is half the measurement of the dog's waist. Cut across the shirt at the line marked for the dog's length (D).

7. As shown in figure 1, draw a curved line connecting points A, B, and C. Do *not* cut the shirt. Pin through the line as shown in figure 2. Check the reverse side of the shirt to make sure there are no wrinkles or folds in the pinning. **Note:** T-shirt fabric is stretchy! Use lots of pins.

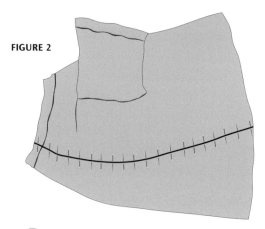

FIGURE 2

8. Use a scrap of the T-shirt fabric to test the tension of your sewing machine's stretch stitch. The correct tension will prevent the fabric from puckering. Insert the fabric in the sewing machine so the points on the Vs of the stretch stitch will point away from the seam. **Note:** If your machine doesn't have a stretch stitch, use the zigzag stitch set to a slightly longer length.

9. Sew down the line drawn in step 7. Trim the excess fabric from the back, leaving a 1/2-inch (1.5 cm) seam allowance. Overcast the seam (page 16) using a zigzag stitch through both layers of fabric.

10. Hem the shirt using a straight stitch, or zigzag over the raw edge to create a lettuce edging.

11. Sewing a ribbon to the collar of the shirt will prevent the collar from stretching out of shape. To do so, cut a length of ribbon to the measurement for the dog's neck plus 1/2 inch (1.5 cm). Pin the ribbon to the outside of the shirt's collar. Use lots of pins; try not to stretch out the collar as you pin. Overlap the ends, folding the top end under to finish. Sew along both edges of the ribbon. Feel free to use a decorative stitch. **Note:** Some breeds have larger heads than others. If you need the extra stretch to get the shirt over your dog's head, leave the collar untrimmed. Slip the T-shirt on your best friend, and take her out to strut her stuff.

Designer: Ann Marie Matott

My
Pillow Bed

"Bliss! We're all curled
up and *it smells*
like our person."

GO FETCH!

46 inches (1.2 m) of purple fleece,
    58 inches (1.5 m) wide
Scissors
Iron
Pins
Sewing machine
Thread
Point turner or similar tool (optional)
22 inches (56.5 cm) of pink fleece,
    58 inches (1.5 m) wide
Tailor's chalk
15 metal snaps, size 14 or 16
Snap-setting tool
Old bed pillow, standard size

Finished size: 32 x 22 inches (82 x 56.5 cm)

*Seam allowance ¹/₂ inch (1.5 cm) unless
otherwise noted*

SIT. MAKE IT!

1. Cut a piece of purple fleece 33 x 23 inches (84.5 x 59 cm) for the front panel of the sham, and two pieces, each 21¹/₂ x 23 inches (55 x 59 cm), for the back. Using the pink fleece, cut a piece 40 x 22 inches (102.5 x 56.5 cm).

2. Make the sham from the purple fleece. Since fleece doesn't fray, you don't have to hem the overlapping edges of the back panels. Lay the back panel pieces of fleece on the front panel with wrong sides together. One back panel piece will overlap the other. Lightly press with an iron to smooth the fleece. Pin 2 inches (5 cm) in from the exterior edges.

3. Use the sewing machine to sew the back panels to the front. Trim the corners (page 14), and turn the sham right side out. *Note:* Because of the thickness of the fabric, you might find it helpful to use a point turner to push out the corners.

4. Lay the sham with its back facing up, and press the seams. Pin 2 inches (5 cm) in from all edges. Use a narrow zigzag stitch to sew 1 inch (2.5 cm) in from the edges of the sham all the way around to make a border.

5. The templates on page 121 give the placement for the snaps. Use the tailor's chalk to mark the placement of the snaps on the sham. Position the stud side of the snaps ¹/₈ inch (5 mm) outside the zigzag border. *Important:* You should set only the stud side of the snaps on the sham; the sockets will get attached to the blanket. Use the snap-setting tool to attach the snaps with the stud sides facing up on the sham's front.

6. To make the blanket, turn the pink fleece under 1 inch (2.5 cm) on both short sides, press, and pin. Use a narrow zigzag stitch over the raw ends to sew the hems. Repeat on the long sides.

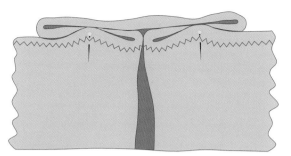

FIGURE 1

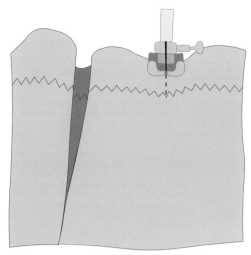

FIGURE 2

7. Make an inverted pleat on one of the long sides (figure 1) by finding the center point on the long side, and marking it with the chalk. Then measure 12 inches (30.5 cm) in from one of the corners. Make a small fold in the fabric at that point, bring it to the center point, and pin. Repeat to make the other half of the pleat, measuring in from the opposite corner. Adjust the folded fabric until both sides of the pleat are centered and of equal width. Pin and press the pleat to make two straight creases at the center of the blanket.

8. Repeat step 6 on the other long side of the fabric.

9. To stitch the pleats in place, first find the center point on one side of one pleat. Then use a straight stitch to sew a 1-inch (2.5 cm) line down from the blanket edge to the hem seam (figure 2). Repeat on the remaining sides of each pleat.

10. Following the template on page 121, mark the placement for the snaps on the blanket, positioning the socket parts of the snaps $1/8$ inch

(5 mm) in from the blanket edge, with the socket on the wrong side of the blanket—the side that will face the sham. Use the snap-setting tool to attach the sockets.

11. Stuff the sham with the pillow, and snap the blanket to the front of the sham. Nap time, anyone?

Reflective
Safety
Gear Set

> **"I just light up when I'm with you. You make me feel so safe."**

Designer: **Candie Cooper**

FOR THE ANKLE CUFFS

24 inches (61.5 cm) of black nylon webbing, 1¹/₂ inches (4 cm) wide

24 inches (61.5 cm) of red-and-silver striped nylon reflective webbing, ¹/₂ inch (1.5 cm) wide

48 inches (123 cm) of black-and-silver striped nylon reflective webbing, ³/₈ inch (1 cm) wide

Scissors

Pins

Sewing machine

Lighter

7 to 10 inches (18 to 25.5 cm) of black hook-and-loop tape, ³/₄ inch (2 cm) wide

Sewing needle and thread

FOR THE LEASH

62 inches (157.5 cm) of black nylon webbing, 1 inch (2.5 cm) wide

45 inches (115.5 cm) of red-and-silver striped nylon reflective webbing, ¹/₂ inch (1.5 cm) wide

1 swiveling snap hook, 1³/₈ inches (3.7 cm) wide in silver finish

3 clear buttons, ³/₄ inch (2 cm) in diameter

5 inches (13 cm) of silver plastic reflective tape, 2 inches (5 cm) wide

3 red buttons, 1¹/₈ inches (3.3 cm) in diameter

Note: The clear buttons should fit snugly inside the recessed area of the larger red buttons.

FOR THE COLLAR

Purchased dog collar made of black nylon webbing, ¹/₂ inch (1.5 cm) wide

10 to 20 inches (25.5 to 51 cm) of red-and-silver striped nylon reflective webbing, ¹/₂ inch (1.5 cm) wide

6 inches (15 cm) of silver plastic reflective tape, 2 inches (5 cm) wide

3 clear buttons, ³/₄ inch (2 cm) in diameter

3 red buttons, 1¹/₈ inches (3.3 cm) in diameter

1 red or white button for charm, 1¹/₄ inches (3.5 cm) in diameter

1 small star- or heart-shaped button

Small, motorized craft tool with a ¹/₁₆-inch (2 mm) drill bit

1 pinch bail

1 split ring, 16 mm

Finished sizes: ankle cuffs, 1 x 6 inches (2.5 x 15 cm); leash, 1 x 50 inches (2.5 x 128 cm); collar, ¹/₂ x 12 inches (1.5 x 30.5 cm)

Note: The reflective gear is made for a medium-sized dog. Depending on the size of your dog, you may need more or less webbing.

SIT. MAKE IT!

ANKLE CUFFS

1. Measure around your dog's ankles. Cut the black webbing into four pieces 6 inches (15 cm) long (or to the desired length). Cut the red-and-silver striped webbing into four equal pieces. Cut the black-and-silver striped webbing into eight equal pieces.

2. For each cuff, lay two black-and-silver pieces on each of the outside edges of the black webbing pieces, and pin. Lay the red-and-silver webbing down the middle of the black webbing, and pin.

3. Using the sewing machine, stitch as close to the edges of the reflective webbing as possible to sew the strips to the black webbing. To prevent the ends of the webbing from raveling, use a lighter in a well-ventilated area to slightly melt the edges.

4. Cut four pieces of hook-and-loop tape, each $1^3/_4$ inches (4.5 cm) long. On one cuff, machine stitch the soft loop side of the tape to the front of the cuff, and the rough hook side to the back. Repeat for the other cuffs.

LEASH

1. Seal the edges of the webbing with the lighter. Starting at one end of the leash, lay the red-and silver webing down the center of the black webbing, and pin. Stitch as close as you can to the edges of the webbing.

2. Thread the webbing through the loop of the swiveling snap hook. Use the sewing machine to stitch the end to the webbing approximately $1^1/_2$ inches (1.5 cm) from the loop. For the strap handle, fold the end over to make a 10-inch (25.5 cm) loop, then stitch the end to the webbing.

3. To make three button reflectors, place a clear button on top of the silver reflective tape, trace around it, and cut out the shape. Stick the tape inside the recessed area of the red button. Place the clear button on top of the red button to fit inside the recessed area. As if you're sewing the button to fabric, take a few stitches through the buttons' holes to secure the layers.

4. Sew two buttons at the bottom of the leash, and one where the strap handle begins.

COLLAR

1. Extend the collar to its maximum length. Cut a piece of the red-and-silver reflective webbing to the length of the collar. Use a sewing machine to stitch the reflective tape to the collar.

2. Make reflective buttons following step 3 for making the leash. Sew them to the collar. **Note:** This project shows three buttons for the collar, but you can make and use as many as you desire.

3. Make the collar charm. As you did in step 3 when making the leash, cut a piece of silver reflective tape, and stick it inside the recessed area of the button you're using for the charm. Lay the small star- or heart-shaped button over the tape, and take a few stitches through the buttons' holes to secure.

4. Drill a hole at the top of the button. Attach the pinch bail at the hole. Use the split ring to connect the charm to the D-ring on the collar. Now, who's ready for a moonlight stroll?

Road Trip
Booster Seat

Designer: **Joan K. Morris**

*" Car?! Car?!
Did someone say car!?"*

GO FETCH!

Foam, cut as follows
- 1 piece, 4 inches (10 cm) thick and 15 inches (38.5 cm) square
- 1 piece, 3 inches (7.5 cm) thick and 15 inches (38.5 cm) square
- 1 piece, 1 inch (2.5 cm) thick and 1 x 15 inches (2.5 x 38.5 cm)
- 2 pieces, 1 inch (2.5 cm) thick and 1 x 14 inches (2.5 x 36 cm)

Spray adhesive

Quilt batting

1½ yards (1.4 m) of upholstery fabric

Pins

Measuring tape

Tailor's chalk or fabric pen

2½ yards (2.3 m) of black nylon webbing, 1 inch (2.5 cm) wide

½ yard (46 cm) of microfiber suede

Scissors

Sewing machine

Thread

Small hole punch

5 metal brads

Sewing needle

Side-release buckle, 1¼ inches (3.5 cm) wide

Finished size: 8 x 15 x 15 inches (20.5 x 38.5 x 38.5 cm)

Note: You may need to adjust the height of the seat (the thicknesses of the foam) for your dog. The seat for this project was made for a miniature dachshund. You can have the foam pieces cut where you buy it.

Seam allowance ½ inch (1.5 cm) unless otherwise noted

SIT. MAKE IT!

1. Cut a piece of batting 30 x 15 inches (77 x 38.5 cm). Cut two pieces of upholstery fabric, one 48 x 11 inches (123 x 28 cm), the other 16 inches (41 cm) square. Cut a rectangle of microfiber suede 4 x 22 inches (10 x 56.5 cm).

2. Position the foam pieces, as shown in figure 1. Use the spray adhesive to glue them together. Lightly spray the seat area and front of the foam with adhesive, and adhere the batting.

FIGURE 1

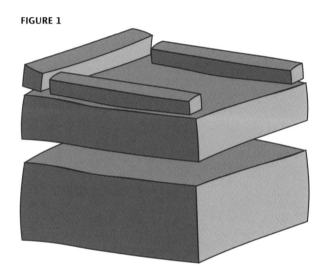

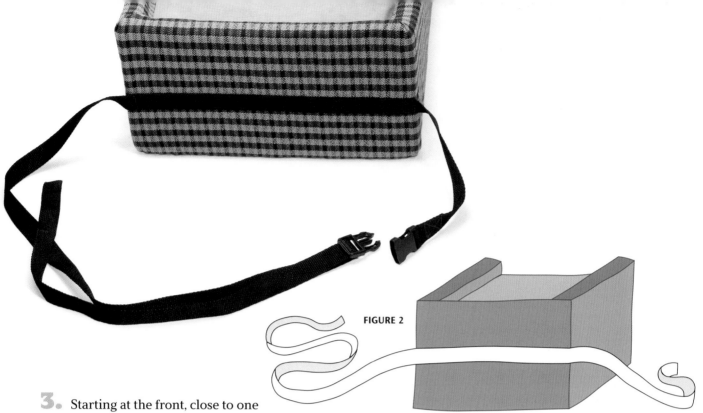

FIGURE 2

3. Starting at the front, close to one of the sides, wrap the upholstery fabric, right side out, around the sides and back of the foam. Adjust the fabric until it evenly overlaps the front and bottom, and covers the sides and back. Pin in place.

4. Find the center of the back, side to side. Use the tailor's chalk or fabric pen to mark the center points on each side. Remove the fabric from the foam.

5. Lay the webbing across the center back of the upholstery fabric, and adjust the length (figure 2). Sixty inches (1.5 m) should extend from the marked point on the left side, 15 inches (38.5 cm) should lie across the fabric, and 15 inches (38.5 cm) should extend from the point marked on the right side. *Note:* The long end of webbing will wrap around the back of your car's front seat. Depending on your car's configuration and where you'll place the booster, you may need to reverse the long and short ends of the webbing.

6. Pin the webbing to the fabric. Machine stitch along both edges of the webbing and across the center points on the sides. To keep the webbing out of the way for now, roll each end and pin them to the fabric.

7. Wrap the fabric, this time wrong side out, around the foam as done in step 3. Miter the corners to shape the fabric to the foam (see Mitering Corners on page 15).

8. Place the upholstery fabric, wrong side out, back on the foam. Lay the microfiber suede, wrong side out, on the seat section and down the front. Pin the two fabrics together where they meet on the inside of the seat, stopping ½ inch (1.5 cm) in from the front corners on both sides. Remove the fabric from the foam, and stitch the suede seat to the upholstery fabric.

9. Evenly space the brads at the edge of the suede, 1 inch (2.5 cm) up from the bottom. Use

the chalk or pen to mark their positions. Use the small punch to make holes at each point, then insert the brads.

10. Place the piece back on the foam with wrong sides out. Pin the remaining length of suede to the upholstery fabric down the front along both edges. Remove the fabric, and stitch.

11. Align an edge of the square of upholstery fabric to the bottom edge of the suede, right sides together, and pin. Sew the pieces together, starting and ending the stitching ¹/₂ inch (1.5 cm) in from both sides.

12. To prevent the seat section from shifting on the foam, you'll need to tack it in place. Turn the piece right side out and place it back on the foam. Roll up the sides. Using the needle and thread, take a few stitches through the fabric seams and the foam around the inside edges of the seat.

13. Roll the sides back down, and turn the seat upside down. Pin the three raw edges of the bottom piece under ¹/₂ inch (1.5 cm) around the edges of the seat. Use the overcast stitch (page 16) to hand stitch the bottom to the seat around all three edges.

14. The long end of webbing will be the adjustable end. Thread it through the glide on the male side of the buckle. Thread the short end of webbing through the loop on the female side of the buckle, bring the end over the webbing, and pin.

15. Check the fit by putting the booster in the car and wrapping the long end of webbing around the back of the car's seat. Adjust the length on the short end to get a snug fit and to give you easy access to the buckle. Re-pin the end on the webbing if needed.

16. Sew the end to the webbing by stitching an X in a square (page 14). Trim the length as needed. Overcast both ends of the webbing with a zigzag stitch to prevent fraying, or use a lighter to singe the ends. Mount the booster in the car, and call around to see who's up for the open road.

In the Saddle

Designer: **Joan K. Morris**

"I'm a dog, a hard-working dog."

Measuring tape

Scissors

$1/2$ yard (46 cm) of corduroy
    upholstery fabric

$1/2$ yard (46 cm) of
    upholstery fabric

Sewing machine

Thread

Iron

Sewing needle

Pins

Tailor's chalk or
    fabric pen

$1/2$ yard (46 cm) of
    black elastic, 1 inch (2.5 cm) wide

$1/2$ yard of black webbing, 1 inch
    (2.5 cm) wide

Side-release buckle, 1 inch (2.5 cm)
    wide in black

Finished size: 20 x 9 inches (51 x 23 cm)

Note: *The saddlebags as made will fit a medium-size dog. You may need to adjust the sizing to fit your pup.*

Seam allowance $1/2$ inch (1.5 cm) unless otherwise noted

SIT. MAKE IT!

1. Cut two pieces of corduroy, each 10 x 21 inches (25.5 x 54 cm), and two pieces of upholstery fabric, each 11 x 17 inches (28 x 43.5 cm), for the pockets.

2. Fold the pocket pieces in half widthwise, right sides together, so the 11-inch (28 cm) edges meet. Machine stitch around the edges of each pocket, leaving a 3-inch (7.5 cm) opening on one of the edges for turning. Clip the corners (page 14) and turn right side out. Use the iron to press flat. Hand stitch the opening closed.

3. To shape the pockets, at the bottom corners measure in 2 inches (5 cm) toward the center of each piece. Sew across the corners at that point. Cut off the corners close to the stitching (figure 1), then zigzag the edges to prevent fraying.

4. Measure in 2 inches (5 cm) from the side and bottom edges of the pocket. Fold the fabric in at that point to bring the edges together, and stitch as close to the edges as possible (figure 2).

5. Position the pockets on one of the pieces of corduroy, right sides up. Pin in place, and topstitch as close as possible along the sides and bottom of the pocket pieces.

FIGURE 1

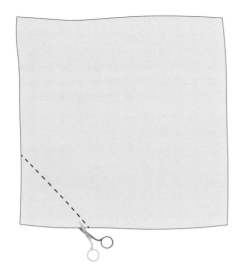

FIGURE 2

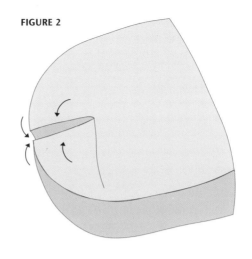

6. Cut a piece of elastic 13 inches (33.5 cm) long. Place the ends of the elastic on the corduroy, right sides together with the raw edges aligned and positioned with the ends of the elastic approximately one-quarter and three-quarters of the way along the edge of fabric. Machine baste in place.

7. Cut two pieces of webbing, each 8 inches (20.5 cm) long. Center them on each of the short ends of the corduroy with pockets. Lay them right sides together with raw edges aligned. Machine baste in place.

8. Lay the remaining piece of corduroy on the piece with the pockets, right sides together. Pin the edges, making sure the elastic and webbing are inside between the layers.

9. Machine stitch around the edges, leaving a 5-inch (13 cm) opening on the long side of the piece without the elastic. Clip the corners and turn right side out. Press flat, and hand stitch the opening closed.

10. Open the buckle. Thread one end of the webbing through the loop on the female side of the buckle. To prevent fraying, fold the ends of the webbing over before stitching in place. Thread the other end of the webbing over and under the glide on the male side of the buckle. Adjust the buckle to fit, and your friend is ready to go to work.

The Diva

This dog, whether large or small, has expensive tastes and settles for no less than the best. Never caught without a fashionable accessory (or two).

Projects

Dressed *to* Frill **Sweater**

"I've got a bad case of the frills!"

Designer: **Rachel Staples**

GO FETCH!

YARN

123 (123, 246, 246, 370) yards (112 [112, 224, 224, 336] m) of (3) lightweight yarn, mohair and wool blend, variegated or solid

Elastic thread, color to match yarn
5mm (size 8 U.S.) knitting needles
5.5mm (size 9 U.S.) knitting needles
5mm (size 8 U.S.) double-pointed needles
5mm (size 8 U.S.) circular needle
1 stitch holder
Yarn needle

GAUGE

9 sts and 12 rows = 2 inches (5 cm) in St st using 5.5mm (size 9 U.S.) needles

Finished size: XS (S, M, L, XL), 10 x 10 1/2 (11 x 12, 13 x 14, 15 x 16, 18 x 18) inches (25.5 x 27 [28 x 30.5, 33.5 x 36, 38.5 x 41, 46 x 46] cm)

Note: The sweater is worked back and forth starting at the neck with a k1, p1 ribbing, before changing to St st. Ribbing finishes the shaped legs. The tail frill is worked in a series of increases on circular needles. The elastic thread and yarn are worked as one.

SIT. MAKE IT!

BODY

1. Using the 5mm (size 8 U.S.) straight needles, CO 40 (42, 46, 50, 56) sts.

2. Working the yarn and elastic thread as one, work k1, p1 ribbing for 2 1/2 (3, 3 1/2, 4, 4 1/2) inches (6.5 [7.5, 9, 10, 11.5] cm). To create a sweater with a rolled neck, increase the length of ribbing.

3. Continuing the ribbing, increase 6 (8, 14, 20, 26) sts evenly across the last row (46 [50, 60, 70, 82] sts).

4. Change to the 5.5mm (size 9 U.S.) straight needles. Beginning with a knit row, work in St st until the garment measures 3 1/2 (4, 5, 5 1/2, 6) inches (9 [10, 13, 14, 15] cm). End with a purl row.

5. Begin the leg shaping. K7 (8, 10, 12, 14) sts (for left front). Turn and work 6 (8, 8, 10, 12) rows in St st, finishing with a knit row. Slip these stitches onto the stitch holder.

6. Cut the yarn and rejoin to remaining stitches. BO 5 (5, 5, 6, 6) sts (for leg opening). K22 (24, 30, 34, 42) sts (for back) and turn.

7. Work 6 (8, 8, 10, 12) rows finishing with a knit row. Slip these stitches onto the stitch holder.

8. Cut the yarn and rejoin to remaining stitches. BO 5 (5, 5, 6, 6) sts (for leg opening). K7 (8, 10, 12, 14) sts (for right front) and turn.

9. Work 6 (8, 8, 10, 12) rows, finishing with a knit row.

10. Rejoin all the stitches on the main needles. P7 (8, 10, 12, 14). Turn and CO 5 (5, 5, 6, 6) sts. Turn and p22 (24, 30, 36, 42) back sts from the stitch holder. Turn and CO 5 (5, 5, 6, 6) sts. Turn and p7 (8, 10, 12, 14) left front sts from the stitch holder.

11. Continue in St st, beginning with a knit row, until the garment measures 8 (9, $10^1/_2$, $11^1/_2$, 13) inches (20.5 [23, 27, 29.5, 33.5] cm), or desired length, finishing with a purl row.

12. Begin the shaping for the tail frill. BO 7(8, 9, 10, 11) sts, and knit to the end. BO 7(8, 9, 10, 11) sts, and purl to the end (32 [34, 42, 50, 60] sts).

13. Dec one stitch at each end of the next row. Then continue decreasing one stitch at each end of every other row until there are 20 (22, 26, 32, 38) sts. BO.

TAIL FRILL

1. Working back and forth on the circular needle, pick up and k44 (50, 60, 74, 88) sts evenly around the tail shaping (starting and finishing at BO edge).

2. Knit into the front and back of each stitch across (88 [100, 120, 148, 176] sts). Purl 1 row.

3. Knit into the front and back of each stitch across (176 [200, 240, 296, 352] sts).

4. P 1 row. K 1 row. P 1 row. BO.

LEG BANDS

1. With the right side facing you, and using the double-pointed needles, pick up 20 (22, 22, 26, 28) sts evenly around one leg opening. Work 3 rnds of k1, p1 ribbing. BO.

2. Repeat for the other leg opening.

FINISHING

Fold the garment in half lengthwise. Sew the center seam starting at the neck. End the seam 1 inch (2.5 cm) from the tail shaping for girls, and 2 inches (5 cm) for boys. Use the needle to weave in all ends.

This sweater was knit with Ashford's Kid Mohair, 82% Kid Mohair/18% wool, 1.75 oz/50g = 123yd/112m per ball

Too-Too **Divine Tutu**

*"Eat your heart out,
Nutcracker ballet."*

Designer: **Shiu Pei Luu**

GO FETCH!

Measuring Tape
$^2/_3$ yard (61.5 cm) of coordinating ribbon,
   1 inch (2.5 cm) wide
Scissors
1 yard (91 cm) of tulle
Sewing machine
Thread
Hook-and-loop tape, $^1/_2$ inch (1.5 cm) wide

Finished size: 13 x 5 inches (33.5 x 13 cm)

Note: Tutus for pups with bigger waists may require more ribbon and tulle.

SIT. MAKE IT!

1. Measure your dog's waist (page 14). Add 3 inches (7.5 cm) to that measurement. Cut the ribbon to this length.

2. Cut the tulle to get a strip that's 5 inches (13 cm) wide and twice the length of your dog's waist measurement. If you have a taller dog, alter the width of the strip for a longer tutu. *Note:* Since you'll gather the length of the tulle strip into the ribbon waist-band, the longer you make the strip, the fuller your Diva's tutu.

3. Set the sewing machine to its longest stitch. Sew a single line along the length of the tulle strip, approximately $^1/_4$ to $^1/_2$ inch (1 to 1.5 cm) from one edge, leaving long thread tails when beginning and ending the stitching.

4. Pull one of the long tails to gather the tulle. The gathered length needs to match your dog's waist measurement plus $^1/_4$ inch (1 cm).

5. Steps 2 to 4 will make one layer. You can attach the ribbon waistband at this point, or make additional layers for a fluffier tutu. The tutu as shown for this project uses three layers of tulle. You can also vary the length of each layer for a different look. With wrong sides together, pin the edge of the ribbon to the tulle, leaving 1 to 1$^1/_2$ inches (2.5 to 4 cm) of ribbon extending from one end of the tutu. Adjust the gathers to make them even, repinning if necessary. Sew the ribbon to the tulle.

6. Fold the ribbon over the raw edge of the tulle, then sew close to the edge of the ribbon through all layers.

7. Turn the ends of the ribbon under for a neat finish before sewing the hook-and loop strips to the ribbon for your closure. *Voila!* You now have a tutu for your prima ballerina!

✚ **SAFETY TIP:** While pretty and light-hearted, this tutu's tulle can be a tempting chew toy for pups. Keep an eye on your ballerina while she wears this sweet outfit—you don't want her to ingest any of the gauzy material.

"**Viva la diva!**"

Mink
Stole
Shrug

Designer: **Joan K. Morris**

GO FETCH!

Pencil
Craft paper
Scissors
$1/2$ yard (46 cm) of mink faux fur
$1/2$ yard (46 cm) of brocade
Pins
Sewing machine
Thread
Measuring tape
$1/2$ yard (46 cm) of leopard faux fur
Needle
Bowl

*Finished size: 29 x 12$1/2$ inches (74.5 x 32 cm)
to fit a medium-sized dog*

*Seam allowance $1/2$ inch (1.5 cm) unless
otherwise noted*

SIT. MAKE IT!

1. Enlarge the template on page 125. Adjust it to fit your dog, transfer it to the craft paper, and cut it out. Use this pattern to cut one piece each from the mink and brocade.

2. Pin the faux mink and brocade with wrong sides together. Baste around the edges of the piece using a $1/4$-inch (6 mm) seam allowance.

3. Measure around the edge, and then add 2 inches (5 cm) to this measurement. Cut a strip from the faux leopard that is 3 inches (7.5 cm) by the edge measurement. (You may need to piece the strip.)

4. Overlapping the center point of the stole's bottom edge by 1 inch (2.5 cm), lay the leopard strip on the mink with right sides facing. Pin in place. When you've pinned all the way around, overlap the starting end of the leopard strip by 1 inch (2.5 cm). Machine stitch the leopard strip to the mink. Clip the curves (page 14).

5. Turn the leopard strip over the raw edge to the inside of the stole, and hand stitch in place, turning the raw edge of the leopard strip under as you sew.

6. To create the legholes, find a bowl that measures approximately $4^1/2$ inches (11.5 cm) across. Follow the template for positioning the holes, and trace around the bowl directly onto the back of the stole.

7. Machine stitch around the traced line. Cut out the circle, leaving a $1/2$-inch (1.5 cm) allowance from the stitching.

8. Measure around the leghole, and add 2 inches (5 cm) to this measurement. Cut two strips from the faux leopard, each $2^1/2$ inches (6.5 cm) by the leghole measurement. As you did in steps 4 and 5, machine stitch each strip around a leghole, clip the curves, roll the strips to the inside, and hand stitch.

"Every diva
needs beauty rest."

Designer: **Joan K. Morris**

Luxurious **Bed Tote**

GO FETCH!

Measuring tape
Scissors
1 yard (91 cm) of brocade upholstery fabric
1 yard (91 cm) of soft upholstery fabric
Iron
Sewing machine
Thread
Pins
4 yards (3.6 m) of 1-inch-wide
    (2.5 cm) white webbing
1 piece of 1-inch-thick (2.5 cm) foam,
    25 x 27 inches (64 x 69 cm)
6 snaps, $^7/_8$ inch (2.2 cm) in diameter
Sewing needle

Finished size: $25^1/_2$ x $27^1/_2$ (65.5 x 70.5 cm)

Seam allowance $^1/_2$ inch (1.5 cm)
unless otherwise noted

SIT. MAKE IT!

1. Using the brocade, cut a piece 27 x 29 inches (69 x 74.5 cm), and another 14 x 27 inches (36 x 69 cm) for the pocket. Cut a piece 27 x 29 inches (69 x 74.5 cm) out of the upholstery fabric.

2. Hem the pocket piece. Turn the long edges of the piece under 1 inch (2.5 cm); press. Turn the raw edges into the folds, creating $^1/_2$-inch (1.5 cm) hems, and press. Machine stitch both hems.

3. Fold the large piece of brocade in half widthwise, with wrong sides together, so the 27-inch (69 cm) edges meet, and press.

4. Fold the pocket in half lengthwise, with wrong sides together, so the hemmed edges meet, and press.

5. Position the pocket over the larger piece, fold to fold, with both pieces right side up. Pin the pocket in place, then machine baste close to the side edges.

6. Cut two pieces of webbing, each 29 inches (74.5 cm) long. Lay the webbing on the piece lengthwise over the pockets, positioning them so they lie 8 inches (20.5 cm) apart, each 4 inches (10 cm) from the center of the piece; pin. Machine stitch as close as possible to each edge of the webbing strips to sew in place.

7. To make the handles, cut two pieces of webbing, each 36 inches (91 cm) long. Lay the ends of one strip, right sides together, over the ends of the stitched webbing at one end of the piece, and pin. Repeat at the other edge using the other cut handle. Make sure the handles aren't twisted, then machine baste in place.

8. Pin the brocade to the upholstery fabric, right sides together. Make sure the handles lie inside between the pieces. Machine stitch around the piece. At the top edge, stitch in 3 inches (7.5 cm) from each corner to leave a large opening in the middle for turning and stuffing. Trim the corners (page 14) and turn right side out.

9. Stuff the foam into the cover, making sure to smooth out any wrinkles and to get a good fit at the corners.

10. Hand stitch the opening closed. Space the snaps along the length of the piece, and sew them in place. *Note:* If you're worried your dog might chew the snaps, use hook-and-loop tape instead. Fill the pockets with your Diva's overnight goodies, and you're ready to go.

Posh Pet-Danna

"I don't go anywhere
without crystals, darling."

Designer: **Candie Cooper**

GO FETCH!

Craft paper
Pencil
Scissors
2 fat quarters of different cotton prints
Embroidery floss in solid and
　　variegated colors
Pins
Sewing machine and thread
Iron
Sewing needle
Iron-on flat-back crystals in colors of choice
Plastic rhinestones (optional)
Fabric adhesive (optional)
Dog collar
Needle-nose pliers
1 two-hole flat-back faceted cabochon
1 pinch bail
1 leaf bead
1 jump ring, 5mm
1 split ring, 16mm

Finished size: 17 x 5 inches (43.5 x 13 cm)

Seam allowance ¹/₄ inch (1 cm) unless otherwise noted

SIT. MAKE IT!

BANDANNA

1. Use the template on page 122 to make the pattern. *Note:* The size as given will fit a 10- to 12-inch (25.5 to 30.5 cm) collar. Increase or decrease the size of the pattern to fit your dog. Use the pattern to check the fit before cutting the fabric, and adjust as needed. Trace the pattern on each of the fabrics, and cut out.

2. Embroider the front as desired, adding stitches that highlight the print. The designer used the satin stitch, stem stitch, and French knots (page 16).

3. Pin the two pieces of fabric right sides together. Machine stitch the two layers together, leaving a small opening. Turn the piece right side out through the opening, and press. Hand stitch the opening closed.

4. Embellish with the iron-on crystals, following the manufacturer's instructions for applying them to the fabric. You can also use plastic rhinestones and fabric adhesive to decorate.

5. To attach the bandanna to the collar, fold the fabric diagonally, right side out. Slip the collar inside next to the fold line. Use a needle and thread to take tiny stitches through the two layers of fabric. *Note:* If you prefer to machine stitch the bandanna to attach it, you'll have to do that before you embellish it with crystals.

COLLAR DANGLE

1. Attach the pinch bail to the top of the faceted cabochon. Using the pliers, connect the leaf bead at the bottom hole of the cabochon with the jump ring.

2. Finish by sliding the loop on the pinch bail onto the split ring and then onto the D-ring on the collar. Take a stroll in the sun, and watch your Diva dazzle!

Sumptuous
Snood

"*That's snood, darling. It's a hood with attitude.*"

Designer: **Rhonda M. Gold**

GO FETCH!

YARN

Color A: One skein of (6) super bulky weight yarn, 100% merino wool, black

Color B: 60 yards (54 m) of (6) super bulky weight handspun, hand-dyed yarn, 100% wool plied with fringy multicolor art yarn, in color combination of choice

8mm (size 11 U.S.) double-pointed needles, 7½ inches (19 cm) long *or size to obtain gauge*

Tape measure

1 stitch marker

Scissors

Jumbo darning needle

Iron

GAUGE

Color A: 9 sts and 14 rows = 4 inches (10 cm) in St st using 8mm (size 11 U.S.) needles.

Color B: Since this yarn is handspun with varying thicknesses, bumps, and coils, the gauge will be close to Color A, but not exact. Take an average, but don't worry about the difference—the quirky nature of the yarn gives the piece its personality.

Always take time to check your gauge.

Finished Measurement : 15 to 16 inches (38.5 to 41 cm) in circumference x 10 inches (26 cm)

Note: The snood is knit in the round on double-pointed needles. The neckband and turtleneck are worked in a k2, p2 ribbing. The neck is knit using the Stockinette Stitch.

BEFORE YOU BEGIN

Measure your dog's neck in three places: the length from the base of the skull to the top of the shoulders; the circumference of the neck around the base of the skull (at the base of the ears); and the circumference of the neck around the base of the neck at the shoulders (as for a collar).

The instructions are written for an average-size dog (refer to the finished measurements). For smaller dogs, decrease the number of cast-on stitches by four stitches for each 2-inch (5 cm) reduction in circumference. Adjust the length of the snood's body to accommodate a shorter neck. For larger dogs, increase the number of cast-on stitches by four stitches for every 2-inch (5 cm) increase in circumference. Adjust the length of the snood's body to accommodate a longer neck. *Note:* Additions and reductions in four-stitch intervals allow you to work the k2, p2 ribbing in the round.

SIT. MAKE IT!

NECKBAND

1. Loosely cast on 32 sts (or multiple of 32 sts +/- 4sts) of Color B. Divide the stitches on three needles (12, 10, 10 sts). Make sure you don't twist the yarn when dividing the stitches. It's important to cast on loosely to prevent the neckband from being too tight when pulled over the dog's head.

2. Join the stitches in the round by using the fourth needle to connect the ends and begin the neckband ribbing. Place a stitch marker on the needle between the 1st and 2nd stitch on the first needle.

3. K2, p2 around, repeating the pattern for each round. Try to keep the gauge as even as possible. Keep tension consistent as you knit from needle to needle. Continue k2 p2 ribbing until the neckband measures 2 inches (5 cm). Cut the end, leaving a 5-inch (13 cm) tail.

NECK

Switch to Color A at the beginning of the next round, leaving a 5-inch (13 cm) tail. Knit every stitch. (When working in the round, all stitches are knit for St st.) Work evenly until the piece measures 7 inches (18 cm) from cast-on row. Adjust the length according to your dog's measurements. At the end of your last round, cut the end, leaving a 5-inch (13 cm) tail.

TURTLENECK

1. To begin the turtleneck, switch to Color B, leaving a 5-inch (13 cm) tail, and knit 1 round. On the 2nd round, begin the k2, p2 ribbing, working loosely (to allow the snood to flare slightly at the shoulder end) until the snood measures 10 inches (25.5 cm) from CO.

2. Bind off all stitches in k2, p2 very loosely, taking care to remove the stitch marker. Use a loose hand when binding off to prevent the opening from becoming too tight and to allow you to easily turn the turtleneck up or down. The lower section of the snood should be wider than the top neck section. Trim the yarn, leaving a 5-inch (13 cm) tail.

FINISHING

1. Use the jumbo darning needle to work the tails into the matching colored wool inside the snood.

2. If Color B has lumps, bumps, coils, fringe, etc., be sure to push them out to the right side of the neckband for maximum design impact. For the turtleneck, distribute these ends evenly on either side so they can be seen whether the neck is turned up or down.

3. Block the snood with a steam iron held a short distance above above the piece. Place a cloth between the iron and the snood to avoid scorching the yarn. Carefully shape the piece, and dry flat.

This snood was made with
(A) Rowan's Big Wool, 100% merino wool, 88yd/80m, 3.5 oz/100g per ball, color 008 Black
(B) FuzzyFiber, 100% wool plied with fringed novelty art yarn, 60yd/54m, color Mum

➕ **SAFETY TIP:** Never leave a snood on an unattended dog; it could pose a hazard.

The Rocker

Full of attitude but irresistibly charming. Up all night; snoozing during the day. A real city dog, uptown or downtown.

Projects

Ana**rchy** Rules T-Shirt

*"Rules?
I don't need no
stinkin' rules."*

Designer: **Wendi Gratz**

GO FETCH!

1 blank doggie T-shirt in black
Pencil
Freezer paper
Craft knife
1 piece of thin cardboard
Iron
White fabric paint
Disposable foam brush

Finished size: This project used a large T-shirt, 17¹/₂ inches (45 cm) long

SIT. MAKE IT!

1. Using the template on page 124, copy the anarchy symbol at a size that will fit on the back of the T-shirt. Trace the symbol on the *uncoated* side of the freezer paper.

2. To make your stencil, use the craft knife to cut around the outline of the symbol, then cut out the pieces inside the symbol. Be careful while cutting to keep all the pieces whole. (Think of it as making a puzzle.) Set the pieces aside.

3. Lay the T-shirt on your work surface, making sure the broad part across the back is smooth. Slide the piece of cardboard into the shirt to prevent the paint from bleeding through.

4. Position just the outline of the symbol, with the coated side of the stencil down, on the shirt. Set your iron for dry—no steam—and make a quick swipe over the paper to hold it in place.

5. Now complete your puzzle. First lay the cutout anarchy symbol within its outline, and press

as in step 4. Then lay all the remaining small pieces inside the symbol, and press.

6. Now *gently* peel away *only* the anarchy symbol from the outline, leaving all the smaller pieces on the T-shirt. Make sure all the remaining little pieces are perfectly positioned, and press again.

7. Use the brush to dab—not stroke—the fabric paint over the stencil. Stroking or brushing the paint will push it under the edges of your stencil, making the finished graphic less crisp.

8. Following the manufacturer's instructions, allow the paint to dry thoroughly, then dab on a second coat and allow it to dry. Carefully peel the stencil from the T-shirt. **Note:** Always follow the paint manufacturer's instructions for drying and care. Depending on the brand, some require heat setting (with an iron or in the dryer), while others require air curing or several days before washing. Take your Rocker out on the town, and you'll make a *real* fashion statement.

Wild Monster Balls

"Lemme at 'em!"

Designer: **Candie Cooper**

GO FETCH!

Sweaters of 100% wool in patterns and solids
Washing machine
Iron
Scissors
Sewing machine and thread
Craft felt in various colors
Needle and thread
Yarn needle and yarn (optional)
Felting needle (optional)
Wool roving (optional)
Tennis ball
Awl (optional)
Felt balls, $1/2$ inch (1.5 cm) in
    diameter (optional)
Loop turner (optional)

Finished sizes: orange and blue monster,
$4^1/2$ x 8 inches (11.5 x 20.5 cm); red monster
$4^1/2$ x 11 inches (11.5 x 28 cm); purple monster,
$4^1/2$ x 14 inches (11.5 x 36 cm)

Seam allowance $1/4$ inch (1 cm) unless
otherwise noted

SIT. MAKE IT!

1. Felt the sweaters (page 11).

2. Enlarge and cut out the template on page 122. Trace it twice on a felted sweater. You can make both pieces the same color or use two different colors, but a solid color works best for the face. The back of the head can be either a solid or a pattern.

3. Make the body by cutting two rectangles out of a felted sweater, each $4^1/4$ x 10 inches (11 x 25.5 cm).

4. Lay the face piece on one of the body pieces, right sides together. Machine stitch the face to the body. Do the same for the back of the head.

5. Cut eyes and a mouth from felt as desired. Hand stitch them to the face. Embellish the face with yarn embroidery if desired, or use a felting needle and roving to needle felt circles for the cheeks.

6. Pin the front to the back with right sides together, and stitch around the edges, leaving the bottom open. Turn the piece, and press.

7. Slip the tennis ball into the head. You can close the head and finish off the body in a variety of ways. See the next page for ideas:

ORANGE AND
BLUE MONSTER

Trim off 5 inches (13 cm) from the rectangles for the body. Slit the body lengthwise (front and back) into an equal number of strips. Tie opposite strips in knots near the tennis ball to close the head. Use an awl to poke holes in felt balls. Using a loop turner, pull the ends of the strips through the balls, then knot the ends of the strips to keep the balls from sliding off.

RED MONSTER

Trim off 4 inches (10 cm) from the rectangles for the body. Slit the tail lengthwise (front and back) into an equal number of strips. Cut the front and back panels of the body into an equal number of strips. Cut a piece from a felted sweater 1 x 6 inches (2.5 x 15 cm). Gather the strips close to the tennis ball, wrap the felt piece around the strips, and tie in a knot to close the head. Tie the ends of some of the strips in knots. Use a yarn needle and yarn to work the blanket stitch (page 16) over some of the ends.

PURPLE MONSTER

Slit the body lengthwise into three equal sections, and braid them. Tie the top and bottom off with a thick piece of yarn or felt. For extra hold, add a few stitches to the yarn holding the braid together at the bottom.

✚ SAFETY TIP: Make sure tennis balls don't pose a choking hazard for your four-legged pal.

Reversible
Flight
Jacket

"*Admit it—flyboys (and musicians) are heartthrobs.*"

Designer: **Joan K. Morris**

GO FETCH!

Measuring tape
Craft paper
Scissors
³/₄ yard (69 cm) of brown faux-leather vinyl
³/₄ yard (69 cm) of lightweight corduroy
Pins
Sewing machine
Thread
7 inches (18 cm) of black elastic,
    1 inch (2.5 cm) wide
24 inches (61.5 cm) of black nylon
    webbing, 1 inch (2.5 cm) wide
Iron
Sewing needle
Tailor's chalk or fabric pen
23 antique-brass finish grommets,
    ¹/₂ inch (1.5 cm) in diameter
Grommet-setting tool
1 black side-release buckle,
    1¹/₄ inches (3.5 cm) wide

Finished size: 20¹/₂ x 22 inches (52.5 x 56.5 cm)

Seam allowance ¹/₂ inch (1.5 cm)
unless otherwise noted

SIT. MAKE IT!

1. Measure your dog (page 14). Enlarge the templates on pages 122 and 123, sizing it to fit your dog. Make the pattern on craft paper, and use it to cut out the fabrics. Cut two backs and two gussets out of the faux leather, as well as a piece 4¹/₂ x 16 inches (11.5 x 41 cm), for the collar. Cut the lining by folding the corduroy in half lengthwise, placing the center back of the pattern on the fold, and cutting it out.

2. Pin the side gussets to the back pieces with right sides together. Ease the curves as necessary. Sew the gussets to the back pieces. Notch the curves (page 14).

3. Pin the back pieces right sides together at the center back, and stitch them together.

4. Fold the collar piece in half lengthwise with right sides together. Machine stitch the short ends (figure 1). Clip the corners and turn right side out, making sure to push the corners all the way out.

5. Lay the collar on the neckline of the back piece, right sides together, lining up the raw edges. Position the ends of the collar 1¹⁄₄ inches (3.5 cm) in from the edges of the neckline on both sides of the back piece (figure 2). Pin, and machine baste.

6. On the right side of the jacket fronts, center the elastic strip with one end on each of the fronts, and pin. Machine baste.

7. Cut the nylon webbing in half to make two 12-inch (30.5 cm) pieces. Position the webbing on the gussets as indicated on the template. Lay the webbing on the vinyl, right sides together, with raw edges aligned. Pin, then machine baste.

8. Pin the lining to the faux leather with right sides together, making sure the elastic and webbing are inside the piece and free of the seam allowances.

9. Sew around the edges, leaving a 4-inch (10 cm) opening along the bottom edge for turning. Clip the curves and turn right side out. Using the iron on the lining side *only*, press the seams flat.

10. Topstitch ¹⁄₄ inch (1 cm) in from the outside edge of the jacket. Topstitch ¹⁄₄ inch (1 cm) away from both gusset seams on the sides of the seams that are closest to the center back. Topstitch at the back seam, ¹⁄₄ inch (1 cm) away from both sides of the seam.

11. With the template as your guide, mark the placement of the grommets on the body and collar of the jacket. Following the manufacturer's instructions, use the grommet-setting tool to attach the grommets.

12. To prevent the ends of the webbing from fraying, use a zigzag stitch to overcast them, or use a lighter to singe the ends. Thread one end of the webbing through the glide on the male side of the buckle (page 11). Thread the other end through the loop on the female side, and stitch the end to the webbing. Get your Rocker's passport, it's time to head for the friendly skies.

FIGURE 1

FIGURE 2

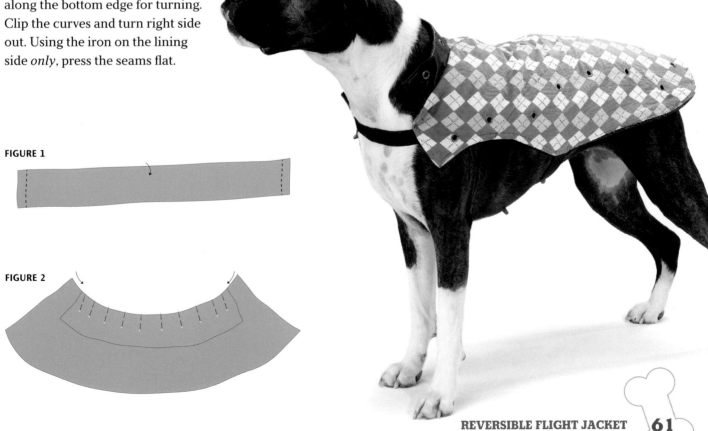

Baaad Dog
Rhinestone Collar

> **"I'm bad to the bone. Uh, by the way, can I have a bone?"**

Designer: **Sue McMahon**

GO FETCH!

Black leather collar 4 inches (10 cm) longer than the size your dog usually wears
Chalk pencil
Utility knife
Cork-back ruler
Leather rotary punch
4 double-cap rivets, medium size
2 D-rings, O-rings, or square rings, in a nickel finish
Rivet setter
1 white 10mm rhinestone rivet
4 white 7mm rhinestone rivets
Cloth scrap

Finished size: 1 x 22 inches (2.5 x 56 cm)

Note: Make sure the width of the D-ring, O-ring, or square ring, matches the width of the collar. Adjust the rivet sizes if needed to fit the width of your collar, and use more rhinestones rivets if you have a really long collar to embellish.

SIT. MAKE IT!

1. Buckle the collar at the middle hole. Divide this buckled length into three equal sections. Use the chalk pencil to mark two lines separating the sections—these will be your cut lines. *Note:* If you want space for more bling, make the section that will be at the top of the collar longer.

2. Use the utility knife guided by the cork-back ruler to cut through the leather at the marked lines. Trim the cut ends to finish as you would the end of a belt (figure 1).

3. Fold one of the ends under 1¼ inches (3.5 cm). Make a mark ½ inch (1.5 cm) from the tip of the folded section. Set the rotary punch to accommodate a double-cap rivet. *Note:* The base of the rivet should be the same size or slightly smaller than the hole. Unfold the end, and punch the hole at the mark through one layer of leather. Refold the end, and mark through the hole to the leather underneath. Punch that mark. Repeat this step for each of the remaining cut ends of leather.

4. Mark the placement of the rhinestone rivets on each section, spacing them to be equidistant from one another. Set the rotary punch to accommodate the rhinestone rivets, and punch the holes.

5. To assemble the collar with the double-cap rivets and D-rings, place one end of a D-ring in the fold at one of the cut ends, positioning the D-rings with the curved sides toward the back section of the collar. Separate the double-cap rivet, insert the shafts into the holes punched in step 3, and snap together.

6. Place the bottom of the double-cap rivet—the side that will face the wrong side of the collar—on the base of the rivet setter. Place the base on a hard, sturdy surface, ideally an anvil, although metal or cement will do. Position the shaft of the rivet setter over the rivet. Using the mallet or hammer, pound the rivet together until it's snug. The rivet should remain immobile when you pinch it.

7. Fold the other side of the D-ring under the next section of collar, and repeat the rivet setting directions in step 6 until the collar is assembled.

8. To set the rhinestone rivets, use the rivet setter, but first place the scrap of cloth in the base to cushion the rhinestones. Insert the rhinestone rivets in their holes, and set them as described in step 6. Put the collar on your Rocker and rock out.

FIGURE 1

Mad Kitty
Squeaker Toy

"Here kitty, kitty, kitty..."

Designer: **Aimee Ray**

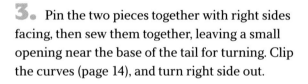

GO FETCH!

Pencil
1 piece of tan twill or canvas,
    15 x 16 inches (38.5 x 41 cm)
Transfer materials
Scissors
Embroidery hoop
Embroidery needle
Embroidery floss
Pins
Sewing machine
Polyester fiberfill
Plastic squeaker

Finished size: 6 x 11 inches (15.5 x 28 cm)

*Seam allowance 1/2 inch (1.5 cm)
unless otherwise noted*

SIT. MAKE IT!

1. Copy the template on page 124. Fold the fabric in half, wrong sides together. Trace the shape on the top layer of fabric. Cut out the cat 1/2 inch (1.5 cm) from the traced exterior line. You will have two pieces. Transfer the embroidery pattern to the right side of one of the pieces.

2. Embroider the face and stripes using satin stitch, split stitch, and straight stitch (page 16).

3. Pin the two pieces together with right sides facing, then sew them together, leaving a small opening near the base of the tail for turning. Clip the curves (page 14), and turn right side out.

4. Stuff the cat with polyester fiberfill and the squeaker. Sew up the opening, and present your Rocker with his new best friend.

✚ SAFETY TIP: Keep an eye on your pooch whenever he or she plays with a squeaky toy. Because the mysterious sound is irresistible to some dogs, they can tear apart a toy trying to find it. Squeakers are a hazard if swallowed.

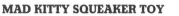

The Good Sport

Always up for a game of Frisbee, a hike on the trail, or a swim in the pond. Can you say fetch? All day!

Projects

Safety Vest. Your best friend will stay visible and safe in this reflective vest. *Page 67*

Frozen Treat Squeaky Toy. After a long day playing fetch, this way-cool chew toy is the perfect treat. *Page 70*

Denim Bone. Turn your old jeans into a new toy for your favorite Good Sport. *Page 74*

Water-Bottle Collar. Make sure your good sport's ready for those enjoyable long walks with his own water bottle. *Page 76*

Sporty Sleeping Bag. Your Good Sport will curl up happily on this foam mattress wherever she is—tent, mountaintop, or snug at home. *Page 78*

Folding Bowl. A drink of water is always close at hand with this nifty bowl that rolls up and goes wherever you and your buddy like to roam. *Page 80*

"Winter, spring, summer, or fall—you've got a friend...**"**

Safety Vest

Designer: **Candie Cooper**

GO FETCH!

Reflective net safety vest
 designed for humans
Measuring tape
Craft paper
Seam ripper
Pin
Scissors
Nylon fabric for lining
Reflective tape (optional)
Hook-and-loop tape

*Finished size: 14¹/₂ x 20 inches
(37 x 51 cm)*

SIT. MAKE IT!

1. Measure your dog (page 14) for the length, girth, and the neck of the vest. Add 2¹/₂ inches (6.5 cm) to the neck measurement. Use these measurements and the template on page 124 to make a pattern, adjusting the fit to your dog.

2. Use the seam ripper to carefully remove the bias tape from the side edges and bottom of the vest, and set aside. Remove the flaps on the sides of the vest, and set aside.

3. Lay the pattern on the vest, aligning the pattern's neck curve with the vest's neckline (figure 1), and pin. Cut out the vest. Lay the pattern on the nylon fabric, pin, and cut.

4. If desired, sew more reflective tape to the vest for even better visibility. There are three extra strips of tape on this vest.

5. With the nylon on top, lay the net and nylon wrong sides together. Lay the bias tape you removed in step 2 wrong side up around the neckline of the vest, aligning its edge to the edges of the net and nylon. Pin the tape to the neckline

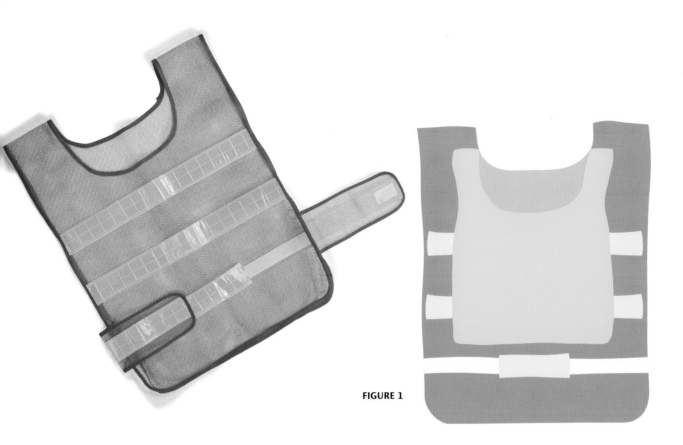

FIGURE 1

through all thicknesses, easing it around the curves as needed, and trim. Stitch the bias tape around the neck, using a $1/4$-inch (1 cm) seam allowance. Fold the tape over the edges of the layered fabrics, and stitch.

6. As you did in step 5, pin and stitch the bias tape to the outside edges of the vest. Start at the top inside of the neckline. Fold the tape in when beginning and ending the stitching to create a neat overlap.

7. Make the belly flaps from the flaps of the net vest, which you cut off in step 2. To determine the length for each flap, first measure the vest back from side to side. Next, subtract this number from the dog's girth measurement, then divide this amount by two. Finally, add $2^1/2$ inches (6.5 cm) to each side to accommodate the overlap for the seam and the hook-and-loop-tape closure. Each flap should be at least $2^1/2$ inches (6.5 cm) wide. Trim the flaps as needed.

8. Sew bias tape to the raw edges of the flaps. Pin the flaps to the sides of the vest, and stitch them on. Sew the hook-and-loop tape to the flaps as indicated on the template on page 124.

9. Allow for a $1^1/4$-inch (3.5 cm) overlap at the neck, then stitch the hook-and-loop tape to the neck flaps. Optionally, you can stitch a rectangle of reflective tape on the front of the closure.

Frozen
Treat
Squeaky
Toy

Designer: **Laura Bersson**

"*If only it were real!*"

YARN

(4) medium weight yarn, 100% acrylic

Color A: 1 skein lime green (MC)

Color B: 1 oz (28 g) tan

Color C: $^{1}/_{4}$ oz (7 g) white

Color D: 1 yd (91 cm) black

Crochet hook, 4.00mm (size G-6 U.S.)

Scissors

Yarn needle

2 stitch markers (optional, but
   very helpful)

Polyester fiberfill

1 or 2 squeakers

*Finished size: 6$^{1}/_{2}$ x 10 inches
(16.5 x 25.5 cm)*

*Note: The toy is worked in continuous rounds
without joining, unless otherwise stated.
Stitch counts in parentheses at ends of rounds
include all stitches and chains. To change color,
work last stitch of old color to last yarn over,
yarn over with new color and draw through all
loops on hook to complete stitch; continue with
new color; carry color not in use loosely along
wrong side of work.*

SIT. MAKE IT!

1. Crochet the treat.

With MC, ch 10.

Rnd 1: Sc in 2nd ch from hook and in next 7 ch,
   ch 2, sc in last ch, ch 2; working along opposite
   side of foundation ch, sc in next 7 ch, 2 sc in
   last ch (22 sts).

Rnd 2: Sc in next 8 sc, (sc, ch 2, sc) in next ch-2
   sp (corner made), sc in next sc, corner in next
   ch-2 sp, sc in next 9 sc (26 sts).

Rnd 3: 2 sc in next sc, sc in next 8 sc, corner in
   next ch-2 sp, sc in next 3 sc, corner in next
   ch-2 sp, sc in next 9 sc, 2 sc in last sc (32 sts).

Rnd 4: Sc in next sc, 2 sc in next sc, sc in next
   9 sc, corner in next ch-2 sp, sc in next 5 sc,
   corner in next ch-2 sp, sc in next 11 sc, 2 sc in
   last sc (38 sts).

Rnd 5: Sc in next 2 sc, 2 sc in next sc, sc in next
   10 sc, corner in next ch-2 sp, sc in next 7 sc,
   corner in next ch-2 sp, sc in next 13 sc, 2 sc in
   last sc (44 sts).

Rnd 6: Sc in next 3 sc, 2 sc in next sc, sc in next
   11 sc, corner in next ch-2 sp, sc in next 9 sc,
   corner in next ch-2 sp, sc in next 15 sc, 2 sc in
   last sc (50 sts).

Rnd 7: Sc in next 4 sc, 2 sc in next sc, sc in next
   12 sc, corner in next ch-2 sp, sc in next 11 sc,
   corner in next ch-2 sp, sc in next 17 sc, 2 sc in
   last sc (56 sts).

Rnd 8: Sc in next 5 sc, 2 sc in next sc, sc in next
   13 sc, corner in next ch-2 sp, sc in next 13 sc,
   corner in next ch-2 sp, sc in next 19 sc, 2 sc in
   last sc (62 sts).

Rnd 9: Sc in next 6 sc, 2 sc in next sc, sc in next 14 sc, corner in next ch-2 sp, sc in next 15 sc, corner in next ch-2 sp, sc in next 21 sc, 2 sc in last sc (68 sts).

Rnd 10: Hdc in next 2 sc, sc in back loops of next 4 sc, (hdc, sc) in next sc, sc in next 16 sc, corner in next ch-2 sp, sc in next 17 sc, corner in next ch-2 sp, sc in next 23 sc, 2 sc in last sc (74 sts).

Rnd 11: Hdc in next st, sc in front loops of next 4 sts, hdc in next st, (hdc, sc) in next st, sc in next 18 sts, corner in next ch-2 sp, sc in next 19 sts, corner in next ch-2 sp, sc in next 25 sts, 2 sc in last st (80 sts).

Rnd 12: Working in back loops only, 2 hdc in first st; change to C in last st made; 2 sc in next 4 sts; change to MC in last st made; 2 hdc in next 2 sts, 2 sc in next 20 sts, skip corner ch-2 sp, 2 sc in next 21 sts, skip corner ch-2 sp, 2 sc in next 26 sts, sc in last 2 sts (150 sts).

Rnd 13: With MC, sc in next 2 sts; change to C in last st made; sc in next 8 sts; change to MC in last st made; sc in last 140 sts (150 sts).

Rnd 14: Repeat rnd 13 (150 sts). Place a stitch marker on this rnd. This is where you'll attach the stick.

Rnd 15: With MC, sc2tog; change to C in last st; (sc2tog) 4 times; change to MC, (sc2tog) 22 times, sc in next 2 sts, (sc2tog) 20 times, sc in next 2 sts, (sc2tog) 26 times (77 sts).

Rnd 16: Working in back loops only, hdc in next st, sc in next 4 sts, hdc in next st, hdc2tog, sc in next 18 sts, (sc2tog) twice, sc in next 18 sts, (sc2tog) twice, sc in next 25 sts (72 sts).

Rnd 17: Sc in next 6 sts, sc2tog, sc in next 16 sts, (sc2tog) twice, sc in next 16 sts, (sc2tog) twice, sc in next 22 sts, sc2tog (66 sts).

Rnd 18: Sc in next 5 sts, sc2tog, sc in next 14 sts, (sc2tog) twice, sc in next 14 sts, (sc2tog) twice, sc in next 21 sts, sc2tog (60 sts).

Rnd 19: Sc in next 5 sts, sc2tog, sc in next 12 sts, (sc2tog) twice, sc in next 12 sts, (sc2tog) twice, sc in next 19 sts, sc2tog (54 sts).

Rnd 20: Sc in next 4 sts, sc2tog, sc in next 11 sts, (sc2tog) twice, sc in next 10 sts, (sc2tog) twice, sc in next 17 sts, sc2tog (48 sts).

Rnd 21: Sc in next 4 sts, sc2tog, sc in next 9 sts, (sc2tog) twice, sc in next 8 sts, (sc2tog) twice, sc in next 15 sts, sc2tog (42 sts).

Rnd 22: Sc in next 4 sts, sc2tog, sc in next 7 sts, (sc2tog) twice, sc in next 6 sts, (sc2tog) twice, sc in next 13 sts, sc2tog (36 sts).

Using yarn needle and D, embroider the face. Begin stuffing treat with fiberfill, and add squeakers. Continue to stuff lightly as work proceeds.

Rnd 23: Sc in next 3 sts, sc2tog, sc in next 6 sts, (sc2tog) twice, sc in next 4 sts, (sc2tog) twice, sc in next 11 sts, sc2tog (30 sts).

Rnd 24: Sc in next 2 sts, sc2tog, sc in next 5 sts, (sc2tog) twice, sc in next 2 sts, (sc2tog) twice, sc in next 9 sts, sc2tog (24 sts).

Rnd 25: Sc in next st, sc2tog, sc in next 4 sts, (sc2tog) 4 times, sc in next 7 sts, sc2tog (18 sts).

Rnd 26: Sc2tog, sc in next 3 sts, (sc2tog) 3 times, sc in next 5 sts, sc2tog (13 sts).

2. To finish, slip stitch in next stitch. Fasten off, leaving a long tail for seaming. Using yarn needle and tail, seam up the hole.

3. Crochet the stick.
With B, ch 2.
Rnd 1: 6 sc in 2nd chain from hook (6 sc).
Rnd 2: 2 sc in each st around (12 sc).
Rnds 3-12: Sc in each st around (12 sc).

4. To finish, slip stitch in next stitch. Fasten off, leaving a long tail for stitching stick to treat. Stuff the stick, then slip stitch it to rnd 14 (marked rnd) of the treat. Ready for some cool playtime?

This toy was made with Red Heart's Super Saver, 100% acrylic, 364yd/328m per skein, 7 oz/196g
(A) 1 skein, color 672 Spring Green
(B) color 365 Coffee
(C) color 311 White
(D) color 312 Black

Denim **Bone**

"A game of fetch?
I love *fetch!*"

Designer: **Wendi Gratz**

GO FETCH!

¹/₄ yard (23 cm) of denim or
    an old pair of jeans
Tailor's chalk or fabric pen
Pins
Scissors
Sewing machine
Red thread
Pinking shears
Polyester fiberfill
Needle and thread

Finished size: 6 x 10¹/₂ inches (15 x 27 cm)

SIT. MAKE IT!

1. Copy the template on page 120. Lay the fabric *wrong* sides together. Using the tailor's chalk or fabric pen, trace the bone on the fabric. Pin along the marked line through both layers of fabric. Take extra care around the bends and curves, using extra pins as needed.

2. Stitch on the traced line, leaving approximately 2 inches (5 cm) open for turning.

3. Use the pinking shears to trim the seam, leaving a seam allowance of ¹/₄ inch (1 cm) around the bone.

4. Stuff the toy with polyester fiberfill, packing the stuffing as tight as possible. Hand stitch the opening shut, using the backstitch (page 16) for extra strength.

5. To get the fringy denim cut-off look, rough up the threads on the pinked edges. Rubbing with your hand or thumbnail should be enough—you don't want to rub away the seam allowance or the seams will pop open.

+ SAFETY TIP: Although it looks good enough to eat, this is a throw toy, and not tough enough for unsupervised chewing.

Water-Bottle Collar

Designer: **Aimee Ray**

"*I'm good for a couple more miles.*"

GO FETCH!

Measuring tape
Fabric
Scissors
Transfer materials
12 inches (30.5 cm) of white elastic,
    $1/_2$ inch (1.5 cm) wide
Tailor's chalk or fabric pen
5 inches (13 cm) of hook-and-loop tape,
    $1/_2$ inch (1.5 cm) wide
Embroidery hoop
Needle
Embroidery floss
Sewing machine
Pins

Finished size: 3 x 24$1/_2$ inches (7.5 x 63 cm)

Seam allowance $1/_2$ inch (1.5 cm)
unless otherwise noted

SIT. MAKE IT!

1. Measure around your dog's neck, then add 3 inches (7.5 cm) to that measurement. This will be the length. Cut two pieces of fabric 4 inches (10 cm) wide by the length.

2. Copy the template for the paw print on page 124. Use transfer materials to transfer the print to the right side of one of the fabric strips, positioning the print as many times as desired.

3. Cut two pieces of elastic, each 6 inches (15 cm) long. The elastic will hold the bottle on the front of the collar underneath the dog's mouth. Use the tailor's chalk or fabric pen to mark the placement of the elastic on either side of the center front, estimating the spacing you'll need to accommodate the size bottle you'll use.

4. Cut two strips from the hook-and-loop tape, each 2$1/_2$ inches (6.5 cm) long, for the closure on the back of the collar. Use the chalk or pen to mark the placement of the tape on the fabric.

5. Embroider the paw prints using the satin stitch (page 16).

6. Machine stitch the rough side of the hook-and-loop tape strips to the fabric at the back of the collar. Shape the pieces of elastic into rings, overlapping their ends, and stitch them to the fabric at the front of the collar, as shown in figure 1.

7. Pin the two pieces of fabric with right sides together. Sew three sides of the collar, leaving one of the short ends open for turning.

8. Turn the collar right side out, and sew the open end. Stitch the soft side of the hook-and-loop tape strips to the fabric at the back of the collar. Press the collar seams flat, and topstitch close to the edges around the collar. Slide a water bottle through the elastic and your Good Sport is ready for that hike you promised.

FIGURE 1

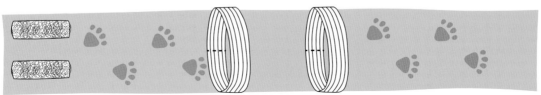

"It's good to be a dog."

Sporty Sleeping Bag

Designer: **Joan K. Morris**

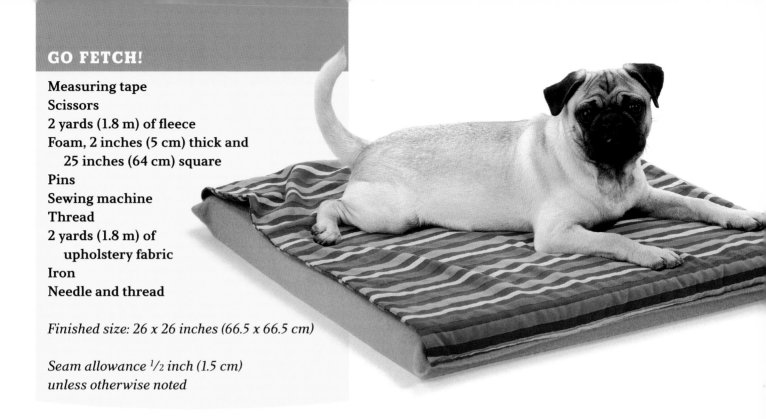

GO FETCH!

Measuring tape
Scissors
2 yards (1.8 m) of fleece
Foam, 2 inches (5 cm) thick and
    25 inches (64 cm) square
Pins
Sewing machine
Thread
2 yards (1.8 m) of
    upholstery fabric
Iron
Needle and thread

Finished size: 26 x 26 inches (66.5 x 66.5 cm)

Seam allowance ¹/₂ inch (1.5 cm)
unless otherwise noted

SIT. MAKE IT!

1. Cut a piece of fleece 29 x 57 inches (74.5 x 146 cm). Cut the upholstery fabric into a rectangle that's 26 x 60 inches (66.5 x 152.5 cm).

2. Wrap the fleece, right sides together, around the foam, centering it so the ends of the fabric meet at the center of one of the 2-inch (5 cm) sides of the foam. Pin the sides together, leaving the end open.

3. Pull the foam out of the fleece through the open end. Be careful to avoid catching the foam on the pins. Machine stitch the pinned sides. Trim the excess fabric, leaving a ¹/₂-inch (1.5 cm) seam allowance. Turn the fleece right side out.

4. Fold the upholstery fabric in half lengthwise, and pin. Stitch around the edges, leaving a 4-inch (10 cm) opening in one of the sides for turning. Clip the corners (page 14), turn right side out, and press flat. Hand stitch the opening closed.

5. Place one edge of the upholstery fabric at one seam of the fleece. Pinch the seam just enough to pin the upholstery fabric to it. Machine stitch as close as possible to the edges of the upholstery fabric. Do the same on the other side.

6. Slide the foam into the fleece. Fold the open end as you would to wrap a package—sides in, and ends overlapping with their corners tucked in on the diagonal (figure 1). Fold the raw end under, and hand stitch across the edge.

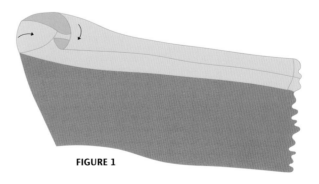

FIGURE 1

Designer: **Joan K. Morris**

Folding
Bowl

"A refreshing drink of water is the perfect follow-up to a hike in the woods.**"**

GO FETCH!

$^1/_2$ yard (46 cm) of upholstery fabric
  for the outside of the bowl

$^1/_2$ yard (46 cm) of waterproof rip-stop nylon

$^1/_2$ yard (46 cm) of one-sided,
  heavyweight fusible web

8 doughnut magnets, 1 inch
  (2.5 cm) in diameter

$1^1/_2$ yards (1.4 m) of fold-over cord trim

$1^1/_2$ yards (1.4 m) of ribbon,
  $1^1/_2$ inches (4 cm) wide

Thread

Scissors

Measuring tape

Iron

Sewing machine with zipper foot

Sewing needle

Pins

SIT. MAKE IT!

1. Cut three squares, one each from the uphol-stery fabric, rip-stop nylon, and fusible web, each $12^1/_2$ inches (32 cm) square.

2. Follow the manufacturer's instructions, and use the iron to adhere the fusible web to the wrong side of the upholstery fabric. Fold the sides of the square in $2^1/_2$ inches (6.5 cm) toward the center, and press each fold. Also press the corners.

3. Place the magnets on the fusible webbing, as shown in figure 1 on the following page. Hand stitch them to the fabric. Start at the center of the magnet and take five stitches on one side, then five stitches on the opposite side. Test whether the magnets hold in position by folding the corners in toward the center to make a box-like shape. If needed, adjust the corners by pulling them in more until the magnets line up.

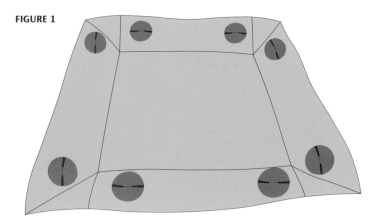

FIGURE 1

FIGURE 2

4. Place the rip-stop nylon over the side of the upholstery fabric with the fusible web, and pin it down. Using the zipper foot, machine baste all the way around the sides of the layered fabrics, $1/4$ inch (1 cm) from the edge.

5. Bind the edges with either folded cord trim or ribbon. You can achieve different looks as follows:

BLUE BOWL WITH YELLOW TRIM

Bind the fabric squares with folded cord trim around all the edges, mitering the trim (page 15) at each of the corners. Use the zipper foot when machine stitching. Once you've sewn around the edges, fold the end of the trim under and overlap the trim where you started.

GRAY BOWL WITH BLUE TRIM

Cut four pieces of ribbon: two pieces, each $12^1/2$ inches (32 cm) long; and two pieces, each $13^1/2$ inches (34.5 cm) long. Pin one of the shorter pieces of ribbon to the upholstery fabric, right sides together with the edges aligned (figure 2). Using the zipper foot, machine stitch $1/4$ inch (1 cm) in from the edge. Fold the ribbon over the edge and pin it to the side of the square with the rip-stop nylon, then machine stitch around the edges. Repeat on the opposite side.

Next, center one of the longer pieces of ribbon on one of the unbound edges, and stitch it down as described above. Before turning the ribbon to the rip-stop side, create a neat corner by folding in the excess ribbon that is at the sides, as if wrapping a gift. Machine stitch in place. Repeat on the opposite side.

The Misfit

You know the type: as sweet as can be, but still a little mischievous. Known to chase the neighbor's cat and snatch a burger off the picnic table, but has a heart of gold.

Projects

SSSly Snake Felted Tug. Great for tugging, this snake toy also helps recycle old sweaters. *Page 84*

Time-Out Crate Cover. A cozy crate cover is perfect for your Misfit's frequent trips to the time-out corner. *Page 87*

On-the-Road Travel Mat. No matter what kind of mischief your Misfit gets into she can follow up her hijinks with a nap on a portable mat. *Page 90*

I'm-Watching-You Throw Toy. Quirky misfits need quirky playthings, and this brightly colored throw toy fits the bill. *Page 94*

Comfy Coil Bed. Use your scrap yarns to create a cute and cozy mat that you can make to fit any size misfit. *Page 96*

"Finally! I've been waiting to chew on that sweater."

SSSly Snake
Felted Tug

Designer: **Candie Cooper**

2 sweaters of 100% wool, 1 in a
    pattern and 1 in a solid color
Washing machine
Detergent
Scissors
Iron
Ruler or tape measure
Tailor's chalk or fabric pen
Rotary cutter and mat (optional)
Sewing machine and thread
Craft felt in white, black, and
    red or pink
Sewing needle
Thread

*Finished size: 4 x 27 inches
(10 x 69 cm)*

SIT. MAKE IT!

1. Felt the sweaters (page 11).

2. Cut the sleeves from the sweaters along the
seam lines, then open the sleeves by cutting them
along the underarm seams. Steam press them flat.

3. The ribbed cuff will become the head of the
snake. From the end of the cuff, measure up the
sleeve approximately 3½ inches (9 cm),
marking the measurement with the
tailor's chalk or fabric pen.

4. Cut across the sleeve to make a strip. Cut
eight more strips from across the sleeve, making
each approximately 2 to 2¼ inches (5 to 6 cm)
long. **Note:** Each snake uses approximately eight
to 20 strips, which is a good size for a medium
to large dog. You can easily decrease the size by
subtracting felt strips.

5. Lay the strips out, starting with the cuff.
You'll see that the strips vary in width. After the
cuff, put them in order of width, more or less,

FIGURE 1

widest first, keeping each centered on its adjoining strips (figure 1 on the previous page).

6. Pin the strips with their right sides together until you have the desired length you want. Use the sewing machine to stitch the strips, then press.

7. Fold the striped piece in half, right sides together, to make a tube, and pin. Stitch the snake, starting at the cuff and tapering toward the tail (figure 2).

8. Trim any excess felt from the seam before turning the snake right side out. Press, making the long seam the bottom center of the snake.

9. Make the eyes by cutting two ³/₄ to 1-inch (2 to 2.5 cm) circles from the white felt. Cut two smaller circles from the black felt for the center of the eyes. Cut two small circles of felt for nostrils. Securely hand stitch the felt to the snake's face.

10. For the tongue, you can use either craft felt (as on the purple snake), or a piece from a felted red sweater (as on the orange snake). To make the tongue, cut a 1¹/₄ x 5-inch (3.5 x 13 cm) rectangle from the felt. Cut a V shape at one end, then taper the tongue down its length as desired (figure 3). *Note:* If you're using craft felt, stitching two layers together will make a more durable tongue.

11. Position the tongue in the snake's mouth, and stitch the opening closed. Finish the snake by tying a knot in the center of the body.

➕ **SAFETY TIP:** Monitor your pup's playtime if he or she is inclined to chow down on anything fabric. Remind your Misfit that toys are for fun, not food.

FIGURE 2

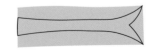

FIGURE 3

Time-Out
Crate Cover

Designer: **Joan K. Morris**

"Sitting in time-out has never been so enjoyable!"

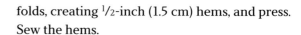

GO FETCH!

Canvas drop cloth, 6 x 9 feet (1.8 x 2.7 m)
Measuring tape
Scissors
Iron
Sewing machine
Thread
Fabric pen
$\frac{1}{2}$ yard (46 cm) of clear vinyl
8 feet (2.5 m) of black cord,
   $\frac{1}{4}$ inch (1 cm) in diameter
8 feet (2.5 m) of black webbing,
   1 inch (2.5 cm) wide
2 rubber stamps, one each of
   a dog and a bone
Makeup sponge
Fabric paint

*Finished size: 18 x 29 x 24 inches
(46 x 74.5 x 61.5 cm)*

*Seam allowance $\frac{1}{2}$ inch (1.5 cm)
unless otherwise noted*

SIT. MAKE IT!

1. Prewash the drop cloth. Measure the crate: the top, two sides, the front, and back. To the top measurement, add 1 inch (2.5 cm) to both the width and length. To the side measurement, add 1 inch (2.5 cm) to the width and $\frac{1}{2}$ inch (1.5 cm) to the length. To the measurements for the front and back, add 1 inch (2.5 cm) to the width and $\frac{1}{2}$ inch (1.5 cm) to the length.

2. You'll save hemming time by preserving the already-hemmed edges of the drop cloth. Using the template on page 120, cut the cloth as indicated. As cut, you will only need to hem one of the edges on the side, front, and back pieces.

3. Use the iron to press a 1-inch (2.5 cm) fold on each of the edges. Turn the raw edges into the folds, creating $\frac{1}{2}$-inch (1.5 cm) hems, and press. Sew the hems.

4. To make the windows, use the fabric pen to draw a 9 x 10-inch (23 x 25.5 cm) rectangle in the center of each piece. Cut an X from corner to corner in each rectangle (figure 1), then cut the center out, leaving a 1-inch (2.5 cm) seam allowance all the way around. Fold and press the seams to the back. Machine baste close to the edge of the window openings.

5. Cut two pieces of the clear vinyl, each measuring 11 x 12 inches (28 x 30.5 cm). Center one behind each of the cut rectangles. Using a zigzag stitch close to the edge, stitch them to the sides.

6. To make the windowpanes, cut two pieces of cord, one 11 inches (28 cm) long, and one 12 inches (30.5 cm) long for each window. Lay them on the vinyl (figure 2), and use a zigzag stitch close to the opening of the window to sew them in place.

7. To make the window frames, cut the black webbing in half. Use one piece for each window. Starting at the bottom of the window, position the webbing to overlap the vinyl approximately $\frac{1}{4}$ to $\frac{1}{2}$ inch (1 to 1.5 cm). Machine stitch the webbing on its inside edge. Miter the corners (page 15). Once you've stitched all the way around, fold the end of the webbing under, sew across the fold, and stitch on the outside edge of the webbing to complete the frame.

8. Stamp the dog and the bone images on the sides and the front, using the makeup sponge to apply the paint to the stamps. (You may find it helpful to first practice stamping on fabric scraps.) Allow the paint to dry according to the manufacturer's instructions.

9. Place the sides and the top right sides together, pin, then stitch.

10. To make the ties for the front, cut the remaining length of cord in half and find the center of each piece. Measure 4 inches (10 cm) in from the sides of the top of the crate cover, and lay the center of the cords on these points. Lay the front panel on the top piece, right sides together; make sure the stamped edge will be at the bottom of the flap when sewn. Sew the front to the top, stitching over the cords. To use the flap, just roll it up, and tie—then go find what mischief your Misfit has gotten into while you were working.

FIGURE 1

FIGURE 2

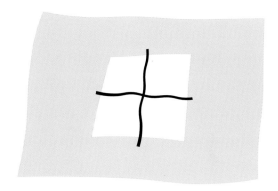

On-the-Road
Travel Mat

Designer: **Candie Cooper**

"Whew! I need a snooze
after chasing that cat."

GO FETCH!

Ruler or tape measure

Scissors

1 yard (91 cm) each of black canvas, printed canvas, and black fleece

1/4 yard (23 cm) of fabric for pocket

Iron

Sewing machine

Thread to match fabrics

Tailor's chalk or fabric pen

Craft felt in off-white and aqua

Iron-on letters

90 inches (2.3 m) of black grosgrain ribbon

1 yard (91 cm) of black nylon webbing, 3/4 inch (2 cm) wide

2 D-rings, 7/8 inch (2.3 cm) wide, in gunmetal finish

2 swiveling snap hooks, 1 3/4 inches (4.5 cm) wide, in gunmetal finish

Finished size: 24 x 35 inches (61.5 x 89.5 cm)

Seam allowance 1/2 inch (1.5 cm) unless otherwise noted

SIT. MAKE IT!

1. Cut a rectangle 36 x 25 inches (92.5 x 64 cm) out of the black canvas. Do the same with the fleece. Cut a piece 36 x 25 inches (92.5 x 64 cm) from the printed canvas; if desired, cut shapes or motifs from the scraps from the printed canvas to serve as appliqués to stitch to the right side of the black canvas later. Using the pocket fabric, cut a piece 17 x 9 inches (43.5 x 23 cm).

2. Turn the top edge of the pocket under 1/2 inch (1.5 cm), and press the fold with the iron. Use the sewing machine to topstitch 1/4 inch (1 cm) from the fold.

3. Divide the pocket into three equal sections, allowing for the finished size with a 1/2-inch (1.5 cm) seam allowance on either side. Use the tailor's chalk or fabric pen to mark the lines.

4. Copy the templates for the bone and water drop on page 120. Cut the bone from the off-white craft felt, and the water drop from the aqua felt. Machine stitch the shapes to the two outside pockets. Add a white highlight to the droplet.

5. Use the iron-on letters to spell TOYS. Following the manufacturer's instructions, press the letters to the middle pocket. *Note:* You could substitute your dog's name or initials for the word.

6. Turn the left and bottom edges of the pocket under ¹/₂ inch (1.5 cm), and press. Position the pocket on the bottom right corner of the printed canvas, and pin. Make the pockets by stitching on the lines marked in step 3, and then stitch along the edges of the fabric.

7. Lay the piece of canvas, right side up, on top of the fleece. Cut the ribbon in half, making two 45-inch (115.5 cm) pieces. Fold the two pieces in half, and pin each to the right edge of the black canvas, one 6 inches (15 cm) from the top and the other 6 inches (15 cm) from the bottom. Line up the folded edges of the ribbons on the edge of the canvas, and lay the tails on top to keep them out of the way when sewing.

8. Cut two pieces from the nylon webbing, each 2 inches (5 cm) long. Thread each piece through a D-ring, folding the webbing in half over the rings. From the left side of the black canvas piece, measure in 2 inches (5 cm) on the top and bottom edges, and mark these points. Position the D-rings on those marks, aligning the ends of the webbing with the edges of the fabric.

9. Lay the printed canvas right side down on the black canvas. Pin the edges through all thicknesses, leaving an opening for turning. Reposition the pins, holding the D-rings and ribbons so you can see them as you sew.

10. Remembering to leave the opening, stitch all sides and press. Avoid ironing in the area of the pocket with the iron-on letters. Turn the mat right side out. Press again, then stitch the opening closed. Tie overhand knots at the ends of the ribbons to prevent them from fraying.

11. To make a strap for easy carrying, cut a piece of black nylon webbing 27 inches (69 cm) long. Thread a swivel snap hook on each end. Fold the raw ends of the webbing under to prevent fraying, and then stitch the folds to the webbing 1 inch (2.5 cm) away from the loops of the snap hooks. Fill the pockets with bones, water, and toys. Roll up the mat, tie the ribbons, attach the strap to the D-rings, and you're ready to make some mischief.

Designer: **Wendi Gratz**

I'm-Watching-You
Throw Toy

"Ooh, ooh, ooh!
I love throw toys!"

GO FETCH!

Paper-backed fusible web
Scraps of fabric with a swirly
    pattern (for eyes)
Scissors
Scraps of corduroy (for body)
Iron
Thread
Sewing machine
Tailor's chalk or fabric pen
Pins
Polyester fiberfill
Needle for hand sewing

Finished size: 4 x 9 inches (10 x 23 cm)

SIT. MAKE IT!

1. Following the manufacturer's instructions, apply the paper-backed fusible web to the swirly fabric.

2. Find two swirls in the pattern that are close in size and color, and cut them out for the eyes. They don't need to be perfect circles—just follow the design on the fabric.

3. Cut two rectangles from the corduroy, each 4 x 9 inches (10 x 23 cm).

4. Peel off the paper backing from the fusible web, and position the eyes near the top of one of the rectangles. Following the manufacturer's instructions, iron the eyes in place.

5. Sew around the eyes using the sewing machine's satin stitch.

6. Use the tailor's chalk or fabric pen to draw a straight line for the mouth, then satin stitch along it.

7. Press both rectangles. Lay them right sides together, and pin. Corduroy tends to shift when sewing, so use lots of pins.

8. Sew the pieces together, using a ¼-inch (1 cm) seam allowance. Leave a 2-inch (5 cm) opening at the bottom for turning and stuffing. Clip the corners (page 14).

9. Turn right side out, press, then stuff tightly with polyester fiberfill. Hand stitch to close the opening.

✚ SAFETY TIP: This is meant to be a throw toy—it's not tough enough for unsupervised chewing.

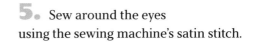

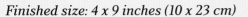

Designer: **Diane Swain**

Comfy
Coil Bed

GO FETCH!

YARN

850 yards (765 m) of ④ medium weight yarn

Polyester fiberfill
Crochet hook, 5.50 mm (size I-9 U.S.)
Yarn needle

Finished size: 18 x 20 inches (46 x 51 cm)

SIT. MAKE IT!

INNER COIL

1. Crochet the tube in the round. *Do not* join the rounds with a slip stitch and *do not* chain 1.

Rnd 1: Ch 2, 5 sc in 2nd ch from hook.
Rnd 2: 2 sc in each sc around (10 sc).
Rnd 3: *Sc in next sc, 2 sc in next sc; rep from * around (15 sc).
Rnd 4: *Sc in next 2 sc, 2 sc in next sc; rep from * around (20 sc).
Rnd 5: Sc in each sc around.

2. Repeat rnd 5 to make a tube measuring approximately 80 inches (2 m). (The size of the mat will vary to fit your dog; adjust the length of your tube accordingly.) Change colors as desired.

FIGURE 1

3. As you crochet, pause every 6 inches (15 cm) and stuff the tube with polyester fiberfill. Don't overstuff. You want the tube to be flexible when coiling and stitching.

4. To finish the tube, you can decrease the stitches to seal it off, or just stop crocheting and stitch the ends together by hand.

5. Begin coiling the tube at one end. Working from the inside outward, stitch the coil to itself with needle and yarn so it keeps its shape (figure 1).

OUTER COIL

1. With its larger diameter, the outer tube will become the border for the inner coil.

Rnd 1: Ch 35; join with sl st in first ch to make a circle.
Rnd 2: Sc in each st around; do not join and do not chain 1.

2. Repeat Rnd 2 to make a tube of desired length. As you did for the inner coil, stuff as you go. Check the length to make sure it's long enough to go around the inner coil. In the example shown, the outer coil is approximately 55 inches (141 cm) long.

3. Stitch the two ends of the larger coil together to make a circle. Place the outer coil around the inner coil. With needle and yarn, stitch the coils together.

This bed was made with scraps of Red Heart's Super Saver, 100% acrylic, 364yd/328m, 7oz/196g per skein

The Social Butterfly

Your best friend, your best friend's best friend, and loves the cat, too! This sweetie really knows how to work a room...or a park.

Projects

Take-Along Kennel Cozy. The Social Butterfly is such a good guest that she brings her own bed when she's out and about. *Page 100*

Talk-to-Me Collar and Leash. Clear vinyl and stamped letters spell out your pup's thoughts for the world to see. Add glitter, photographs, and beads for fun. *Page 103*

Warm and Woolly Crocheted Sweater. Dress your little sweetie to the nines in this darling crocheted sweater, perfect for a party in the park. *Page 106*

Stripes Collar and Leash. Social Butterflies agree—taking care of the Earth is the trend to follow. This project uses cotton fabric and recycled hardware. *Page 109*

Tug for Two. Your pooch is always ready for fun with friends, and this chew toy is perfectly suited for a two-dog game of tug. *Page 113*

Tag Silencers. Tame those jingly dog tags with these personalized tag silencers. *Page 116*

Take-Along
Kennel Cozy

Designer: **Angela Bate**

"*I like my bed better to-go.*"

GO FETCH!

YARN

2 large balls of ③ lightweight yarn, cotton, one each in color A (aqua) and color B (natural)

Crochet hook, size 6mm (size J-10 U.S.)
Scissors
1yd/91cm cotton batting
1yd/91cm new or vintage fabric
Felt scrap, at least 2 inches (5 cm) square
Iron
Pins
Sewing needle
Embroidery floss
10 to 12 buttons, vintage or new
Tailor's chalk or fabric pen
60 inches (1.5 m) of grosgrain ribbon, ¼ inch (6 mm) wide
Thread
Sewing machine (optional)

GAUGE

11 dc = 4 inches (10 cm)

Always take time to check your gauge.

Finished size: 16 x 29 inches (41 x 74.5 cm)

SIT. MAKE IT!

1. Crochet the mat. *Note:* if needed, adjust the number of chain stitches to make a mat that will fit your kennel.

Holding one strand each of A and B together, ch 46.

Row 1: Dc in 4th ch from hook (beginning ch counts as first dc) and each remaining ch across (44 dc).

Row 2: Ch 3 (counts as dc), turn, dc in each st across.

Repeat row 2 until the mat measures approximately 29 inches (74.5 cm) from beginning. Fasten off, leaving at least a 2-inch (5 cm) tail.

2. Cut two pieces of batting, each 15½ x 28 inches (39.5 x 72 cm); the batting should lie just slightly inside the edges of the crochet. Cut a piece of fabric 18 x 31 inches (46 x 79.5 cm), and cut four pieces of felt, each 1 inch (2.5 cm) square.

3. Lay both pieces of batting on the crochet, tucking the yarn tails inside.

4. Fold the edges of the fabric under ½ inch (1.5 cm), and use the iron to press. Lay the fabric over the batting, and pin in place.

5. Thread the needle with two strands of the embroidery floss. Sew the fabric to the crochet (figure 1) by working the blanket stitch (see page 16) around the folded edges of the fabric, taking care that the stitches do not show on the crochet side of the cozy.

FIGURE 1

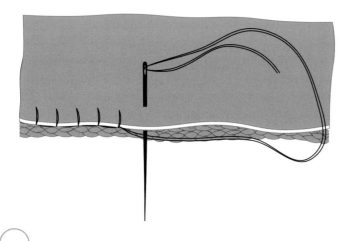

6. Position the buttons as desired on the fabric (randomly, but evenly spaced), and mark their placement using the tailor's chalk or fabric pen. Use the embroidery floss to sew on the buttons. *Note:* If you sew up from the crochet layer, you can hide your knots between the layers of batting and fabric.

7. Fold the ribbon in half, and center it on one of the short edges of the crochet. Sew the folded end of the ribbon to the mat by hand or use a sewing machine for extra durability.

8. Position one end of the ribbon between two of the felt squares, and sew around the square, then sew an X in the square (see page 14) to secure. Repeat on the other end of the ribbon. Roll up the mat, tie the ribbon in a bow, and your pet is ready to travel in style!

This cozy was made with Bernat's Handicrafter Cotton, 100% cotton, 80yds/72m, 1.75oz/50g per ball, colors Aqua and Natural

"I wear my heart on my sleeve—or, in this case, on my collar."

Designer: **Wendi Gratz**

Talk-to-Me
Collar
and
Leash

GO FETCH!

Tape measure
1/4 yard (23 cm) of clear vinyl
Scissors
1 sheet of white cardstock
Alphabet rubber stamps
Ink stamp pad
Clothespins
Sewing machine
Thread
Side-release buckle, 3/4 inch (2 cm) wide
Metal D-ring, 3/4 inch (2 cm) wide
Swiveling snap hook, 3/4 inch (2 cm) wide

Finished size: collar, 3/4 x 18 inches (2 x 46 cm); leash, 3/4 x 46 inches (2 x 118 cm)

SIT. MAKE IT!

1. Measure your dog's neck (page 14). Add 3 1/2 inches (9 cm) to this length. Cut a strip of vinyl that's 2 inches (5 cm) wide by this measurement.

2. Cut another strip of vinyl 54 x 2 inches (138.5 x 5 cm) for the leash.

3. Cut 5/8-inch (1.7 cm) squares from the cardstock. Use the alphabet stamps and ink to print the letters for your messages. For the leash, stamp the paper on the front and back so you can read the message from both sides.

4. Assemble the collar. Turn one of the long sides of the vinyl strip under 1/2 inch (1.5 cm). *Note:* You can't press vinyl with an iron; finger-pressing and creasing it with a thumbnail will usually hold it in place.

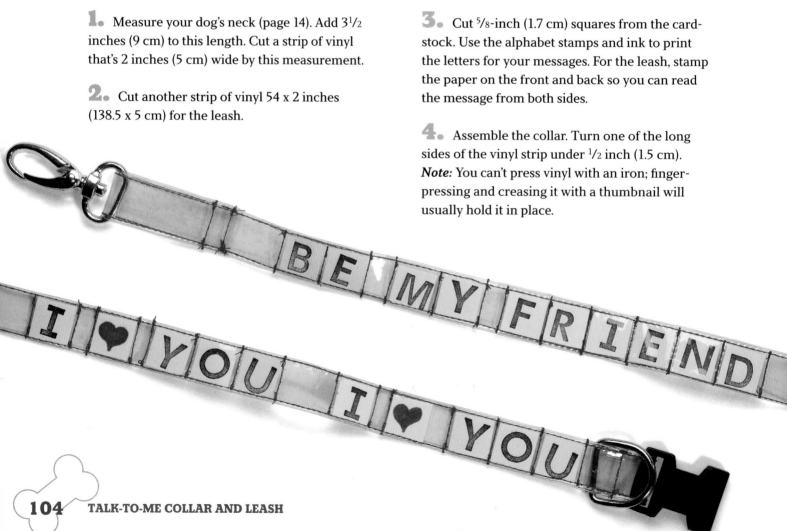

5. Turn the other long side under, lining up its edge even with the fold line. You should be left with a folded strip of vinyl ³/₄ inch (2 cm) wide.

6. Open the vinyl strip, and place the letters in the fold, spelling out your message. In order to attach the buckle, leave at least 1 inch (2.5 cm) of vinyl free from the letters at one end of the collar and 2¹/₂ inches (6.5 cm) free at the other end. There should be a little space between each letter for the stitching that will separate them.

7. Fold the vinyl over the letters when you're satisfied with their placement. Clip the clothespins to the outside of the vinyl to prevent the letters from shifting.

8. Machine stitch between each letter, removing the clothespins as you stitch each short row. Trim the loose ends of thread. *Note:* Vinyl usually sews well with a standard presser foot, but if it sticks, use a plastic-coated foot or place tissue paper under the vinyl while stitching.

9. Stitch each of the long sides of the collar close to the folds. When finished, each letter should be surrounded by stitching.

10. On the end of the collar that has 1 inch (2.5 cm) empty of letters, thread the vinyl over and under the glide on the male end of the buckle. Stitch the end to the collar approximately 1 inch (2.5 cm) from where it loops over the glide.

11. On the other end of the collar that has 2¹/₂ inches (6.5 cm) empty of letters, thread on the D-ring. Thread the end of the vinyl over the loop on the female side of the buckle, then loop the end back over the D-ring. Sew the end to the collar, stitching in between the loop on the buckle and the D-ring.

12. To make the leash, repeat steps 3 to 9 for folding the vinyl, adding the letters, and stitching. Leave at least 1 inch (2.5 cm) of vinyl free of letters at one end of the leash, and 16 inches (41 cm) free on the other end.

13. On the end of the leash that has 1 inch (2.5 cm) empty of letters, thread the vinyl over the loop on the swiveling snap hook, and stitch the end to the collar. For the strap handle, fold the end to make an 8-inch (20.5 cm) loop, and then stitch the end to the leash. Ready for a walk?

Warm and Woolly Crocheted Sweater

"I'm so warm and cozy I could stay out and play all day."

Designer: **Amanda Rydell**

GO FETCH!

YARN

1 skein of **4** medium weight yarn, 100% wool

Tape measure
Crochet hook, 2.75mm (size C-2 U.S.)
Stitch marker
Scissors
Wool felt
Needle
Thread
Button or beads

*Finished size: S (M, L), 11 x 8 1/2
(14 x 10$^{1}/_{2}$, 15 x 13$^{1}/_{2}$) inches
(28 x 22 [36 x 27, 38.5 x 34.5] cm)*

SIT. MAKE IT!

BODY

1. Measure your dog's girth and length (page 14).

2. Use the crochet hook and yarn to make a chain as long as the measurement for your dog's girth.

3. Crochet sweater.
Row 1: Sc in 2nd ch from hook and each remaining ch across.
Row 2: Ch 1, turn, sc in each st across.
Row 3: Ch 1, turn, sc in first 2 sts; *dc in next st, sc in next st; rep from * across.
Row 4: Ch 1, turn, sc in each st across.
Row 5: Ch 1, turn, sc in first st, *dc in next st, sc in next st; rep from * across.
Notes: Beginning row 3 with 2 sc stitches and row 5 with 1 sc staggers the stitches in the pattern to create the texture. Some rows may end halfway through a repetition.
Repeat rows 2–5 until the body section is almost as long as your dog, leaving 5 rows for the neck of the sweater. Do not fasten off.

4. Crochet neckband.
Note: For this section of the sweater, you work in the round (do not turn your work at the end of a round) and decrease by skipping sts in two of the rounds to shape the neck.

Rnd 1: Ch 3, turn, *dc in next 6 sts, skip next st, dc in next 6 sts; rep from * around, ending rnd with number of dc sts needed to reach end.
Rnd 2: Do not ch, curve piece so that you can work first st in first st of rnd 1, *dc in next 5 sts, skip next st, dc in next 5 sts; rep from * around, ending rnd with number of dc sts needed to reach end.
Rnds 3 and 4: Dc in each st around.
Rnd 5: Sc in each st around.

5. Finish with slip st in next st. Fasten off, leaving a long tail, and weave the end into the crochet.

SEAMING THE BODY

1. Turn the sweater inside out. You'll need to leave an opening for your dog's legs. Measure your dog from the center front neck to just behind the front legs. Place a marker at this location on the front edge of the sweater.

2. To seam, start at the marker (leaving edges open between neck and marker), and join the front edges with sl st worked through both edges. End the seaming 1 to 1$^{1}/_{2}$ inches (2.5 to 4 cm) from the bottom edge.

FLOWER

1. Using the template on page 120, cut a flower from the felt. Cut a small circle for the center of the flower. Stitch the circle to the flower. Embellish the flower with buttons or beads. (Different options are shown at left.)

2. Sew the flower to the upper right of the sweater. Your Social Butterfly is now ready to greet the public in style.

This sweater was made with Ella Rae Classic, 100% wool, 219yd/197m, 3.5 oz/100g per ball, color #20 Green Turquoise (page 106), color #52 True Pink (page 107)

✚ **SAFETY TIP:** Keep an eye on your pup when he or she is wearing an article of clothing so you can prevent it from getting tangled or caught.

Stripes Collar and Leash

"I can't wait to show my friends this snazzy new set!"

Designer: **Ann Marie Matott**

GO FETCH!

Cotton webbing, 1 inch (2.5 cm) wide
Fusible web, ⁵⁄₈ inch (1.6 cm) wide
Scissors
Iron
Thread
Sewing machine
¹⁄₂ to 1 yard (46 to 91 cm) of cotton fabric
Collar hardware, 1 side-release buckle,
    1¹⁄₄ inch (3.5 cm) wide; 1 metal
    D-ring, 1¹⁄₄ inch (3.5 cm) wide
Leash hardware, 1 swiveling snap hook,
    1¹⁄₄ inch (3.5 cm) wide
Fray retardant
Decorative button (optional)
Adhesive/sealant (optional)

*Note: For the collar, you'll need approximately
23 inches (59 cm) of webbing and fusible web
to fit a 10- to 14-inch (25.5 to 36 cm) neck, and
approximately 29 inches (74.5 cm) to fit a
15- to 20-inch (38.5 to 51 cm) neck. For a
larger collar, adjust the length as needed.*

*For the leash, you'll need approximately
62 inches (1.5 m) of webbing and fusible
web to make a 4-foot (1.2 m) leash. For a
longer leash, adjust the length as needed.*

*Finished size: collar, 1 x 17 inches
(2.5 x 43.5 cm); leash, 1 x 48 inches
(2.5 x 123 cm)*

SIT. MAKE IT!

FABRIC-COVERED WEBBING

1. Determine the length you need for your size
collar/leash. Cut the webbing and fusible web to
length. If you're making a collar and leash set, you
can save time by adding the lengths together so
you can sew all the fabric to the webbing at one
time, and then cut to size as needed.

2. Cut the cotton fabric on the diagonal (also
known as the bias) into 1³⁄₄-inch (4.5 cm) strips.
Sew the strips together using a 45° angled seam
(figure 1). Press the seams in one direction.

3. Lay the fabric right side up, then lay the
webbing over it. Approximately ³⁄₈ inch (1 cm)
of the fabric should extend from behind the
webbing (figure 2). Sew ¹⁄₈ inch (3 mm) in from
the left edge of the webbing. *Note:* The webbing
is thick, so sew slowly to help keep the stitches
in line. Fold the fabric over the webbing with the
right side up. Press.

4. Fold the remaining raw edge of the fabric under to fit the width of the webbing, and press.

5. Lay the fusible web between the fabric and the webbing. Press, following the manufacturer's instructions for applying the fusible web. *Note:* Working in 6-inch (15 cm) sections when pressing will give you more control over the fusing process.

6. Topstitch the fabric on the webbing $^1/_8$ inch (3 mm) in from each edge. If you've combined lengths for the collar and leash, after stitching, cut the decorated webbing into the lengths you need.

COLLAR

1. Fold one end of the fabric-covered webbing under $^1/_2$ inch (1.5 cm), and press. Thread the webbing through the wide-mouth glide. Overlap the folded edge 1 inch (2.5 cm) onto the webbing. Stitch a square around the edges of the folded overlap through all thicknesses, then stitch an X inside the square (page 14).

2. Thread the raw end of the webbing through the glide on the buckle's male side, then pass the webbing through the wide-mouth glide (figure 3).

FIGURE 1

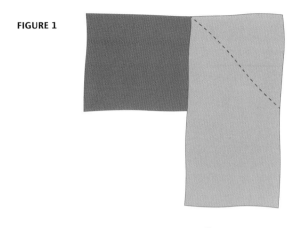

FIGURE 2

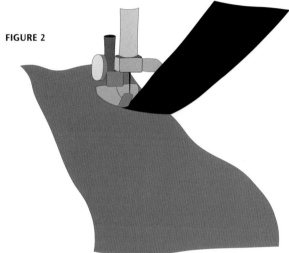

FIGURE 3

FIGURE 4

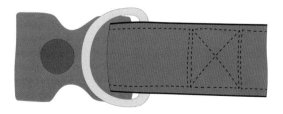

STRIPES COLLAR AND LEASH **111**

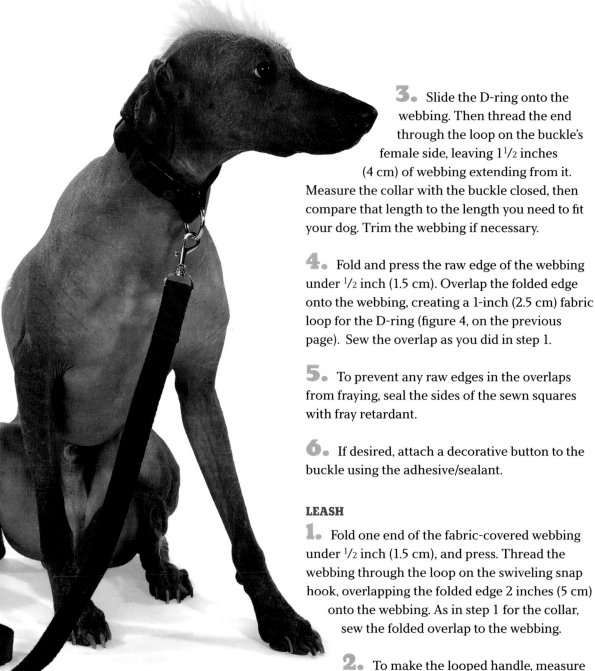

3. Slide the D-ring onto the webbing. Then thread the end through the loop on the buckle's female side, leaving 1$\frac{1}{2}$ inches (4 cm) of webbing extending from it. Measure the collar with the buckle closed, then compare that length to the length you need to fit your dog. Trim the webbing if necessary.

4. Fold and press the raw edge of the webbing under $\frac{1}{2}$ inch (1.5 cm). Overlap the folded edge onto the webbing, creating a 1-inch (2.5 cm) fabric loop for the D-ring (figure 4, on the previous page). Sew the overlap as you did in step 1.

5. To prevent any raw edges in the overlaps from fraying, seal the sides of the sewn squares with fray retardant.

6. If desired, attach a decorative button to the buckle using the adhesive/sealant.

LEASH

1. Fold one end of the fabric-covered webbing under $\frac{1}{2}$ inch (1.5 cm), and press. Thread the webbing through the loop on the swiveling snap hook, overlapping the folded edge 2 inches (5 cm) onto the webbing. As in step 1 for the collar, sew the folded overlap to the webbing.

2. To make the looped handle, measure 8$\frac{1}{2}$ inches (22 cm) in from the end, then fold the end to the webbing and pin in place (see figure 6). Measure the length of the leash from the end of the swiveling snap hook to the end of the handle. Trim to size if needed.

3. Fold the raw end of the webbing under $\frac{1}{2}$ inch (1.5 cm) and sew to the webbing, stitching as you did in step 1 for the collar.

Tug *for* Two

Designer: **Wendi Gratz**

"*Anybody want to join?
This toy's for sharing!*"

GO FETCH!

12 yards (11 m) of 6 mm macramé cord
Lighter or matches
Duct tape
Awl or paring knife
2 mini tennis balls, each 2 inches
    (5 cm) in diameter
Large-eye upholstery needle at least
    2 inches (5 cm) long
Pliers

Finished size: 2¹/₂ x 28¹/₂ inches (6.5 x 73 cm)

SIT. MAKE IT!

1. Cut two lengths of macramé cord, each 3 feet (91 cm) long. Cut two lengths of cord each 15 feet (4.5 m) long. Prevent the ends from fraying by melting them with the lighter. Work in a well-ventilated area, and make sure to protect your hands from the melting plastic.

2. Gather all four cords, and use an overhand knot to tie them together at one end.

3. Tape the knotted end of the cords to your work surface to hold it in place. Position the cords with the two short ones in the middle and the two long ones pulled out to the left and right.

4. Macramé a twist stitch. (If you've never macraméd, don't worry. This is a really simple repeating stitch.) Start by placing the right cord over the two center cords (figure 1). Run the left cord under the tail of the right cord, then under the two center cords, and finally over the loop created by the right cord (figure 2). Pull the tails as tight as you can. Repeat until you have 8 inches (20.5 cm) of twist.

5. Using the awl or paring knife, poke a hole in opposite sides of a mini tennis ball. You just made a bead! Make another bead using the second tennis ball.

6. Using the needle, thread the center cords through the holes in one of the tennis balls. The rubber in the balls tends to grab whatever you're

threading, so you may need to use the pliers to pull the needle and thread through. You may also find it easier to thread one cord at a time. Pull the tennis ball snug to the twist.

FIGURE 1

7. Repeat step 4 until you have another 6 inches (15 cm) of twist after the ball. Pretend as if the tennis ball isn't even there when making the first knot after threading the ball—the cords will simply frame each side.

8. Thread on the second tennis ball, and repeat step 4 until you've made another 8 inches (20.5 cm) of twist.

FIGURE 2

9. Tie the ends using an overhand knot, trim, and melt the cut ends to seal. The macramé is durable enough for unsupervised chewing, giving your canine companion something to do when her social calendar is empty. Tug away!

Tag
Silencers

"Let's get one
for the cat, too."

Designer: **Joan K. Morris**

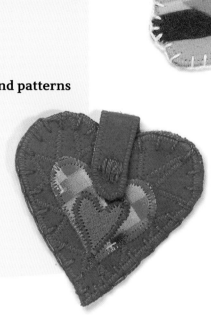

GO FETCH!

Paper and pencil
Scissors
Paper-backed fusible web
Iron
Craft felt in assorted colors
Cotton fabric in assorted colors and patterns
Sewing machine
Thread
Needle
Small snaps
Embroidery needle
Embroidery floss

Finished size: each approximately 2 1/2 x 3 inches (6.5 x 7.5 cm)

SIT. MAKE IT!

1. Enlarge the templates on page 125. Cut them out and set aside. (Note that each silencer has a front and back.)

2. Following the manufacturer's instructions, use the iron to apply the paper-backed fusible web to one side of the craft felt. Don't peel the paper away. When the fabric is cool, trace the templates—including a front and back for each—onto the fusible web's paper backing. Cut out the designs from the felt.

3. Remove the paper from the back of the felt, and use the iron to adhere the shapes to pieces of the cotton fabric. Cut away any excess fabric, trimming it to the shape of the felt.

4. Use the paper-backed fusible web to apply felt appliqués as desired to the front of the tag.

5. Use the sewing machine to zigzag around the appliqués. You can also zigzag stripes on the cat's face. Embroider French knots (page 16) for sesame seeds on the top of the burger bun. Zigzag around the top edges of the front and back of each shape.

6. With cotton sides facing, lay the front and back for each silencer together. Use the zigzag stitch around the side edges to sew the front to the back. Leave the tops open so you can slip in the tags later.

7. Sew a snap onto the tab of the back piece and to the front of the silencer.

8. Using embroidery floss, work the blanket stitch (page 16) around the edge of each piece. To hide the stitching for the snap on the front of the tab, embroider a dot over the stitches using the satin stitch (page 16).

There's a tag silencer for every personality type in this book. Can you guess which one is which?

Templates

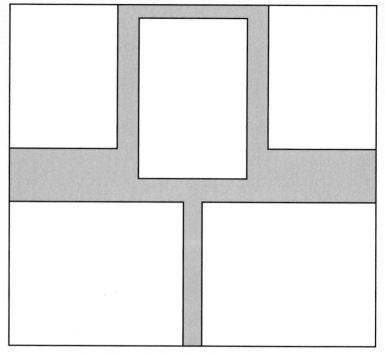

TIME-OUT CRATE COVER, PAGE 87
Lay out pieces as shown

WARM AND WOOLLY SWEATER,
PAGE 106
Actual size
Flower

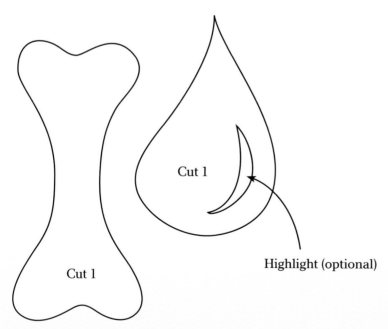

Cut 1

Cut 1

Highlight (optional)

ON-THE-ROAD TRAVEL MAT, PAGE 90
Enlarge 200%

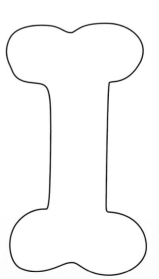

DENIM BONE, PAGE 74
Enlarge 400% or size as desired
Cut 2

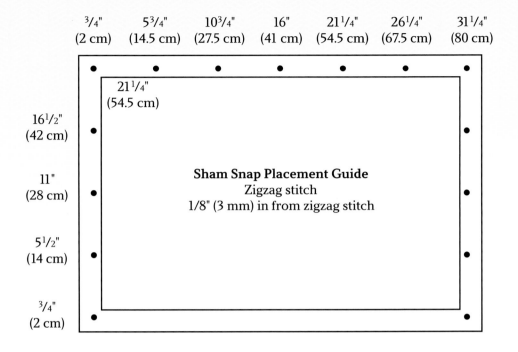

³/₄" (2 cm)   5³/₄" (14.5 cm)   10³/₄" (27.5 cm)   16" (41 cm)   21¹/₄" (54.5 cm)   26¹/₄" (67.5 cm)   31¹/₄" (80 cm)

21¹/₄"
(54.5 cm)

16¹/₂"
(42 cm)

11"
(28 cm)

5¹/₂"
(14 cm)

³/₄"
(2 cm)

Sham Snap Placement Guide
Zigzag stitch
1/8" (3 mm) in from zigzag stitch

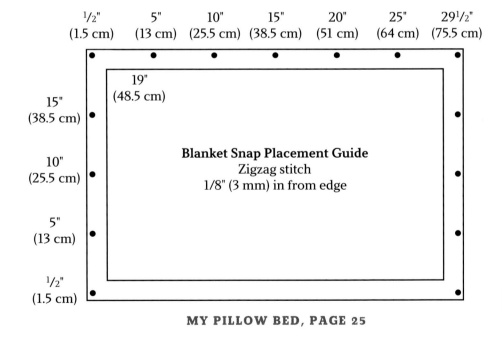

¹/₂" (1.5 cm)   5" (13 cm)   10" (25.5 cm)   15" (38.5 cm)   20" (51 cm)   25" (64 cm)   29¹/₂" (75.5 cm)

19"
(48.5 cm)

15"
(38.5 cm)

10"
(25.5 cm)

5"
(13 cm)

¹/₂"
(1.5 cm)

Blanket Snap Placement Guide
Zigzag stitch
1/8" (3 mm) in from edge

MY PILLOW BED, PAGE 25

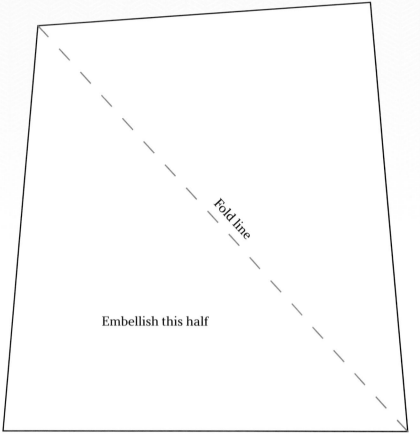

Fold line

Embellish this half

POSH PET-DANNA, PAGE 48
Enlarge 200% or size as desired

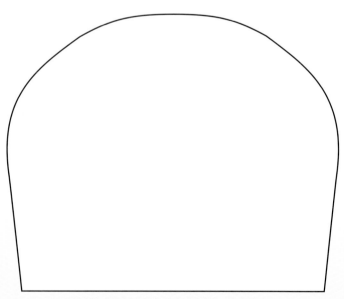

WILD MONSTER BALLS, PAGE 56
Enlarge 133%
Cut 2

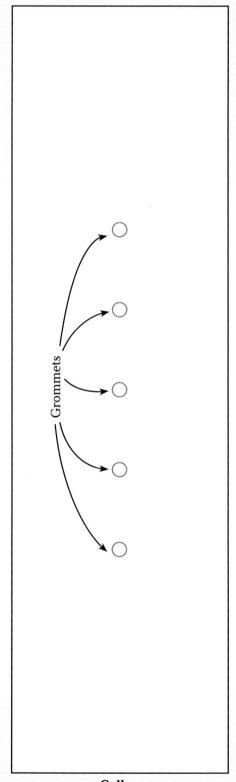

Grommets

Collar
Cut 1

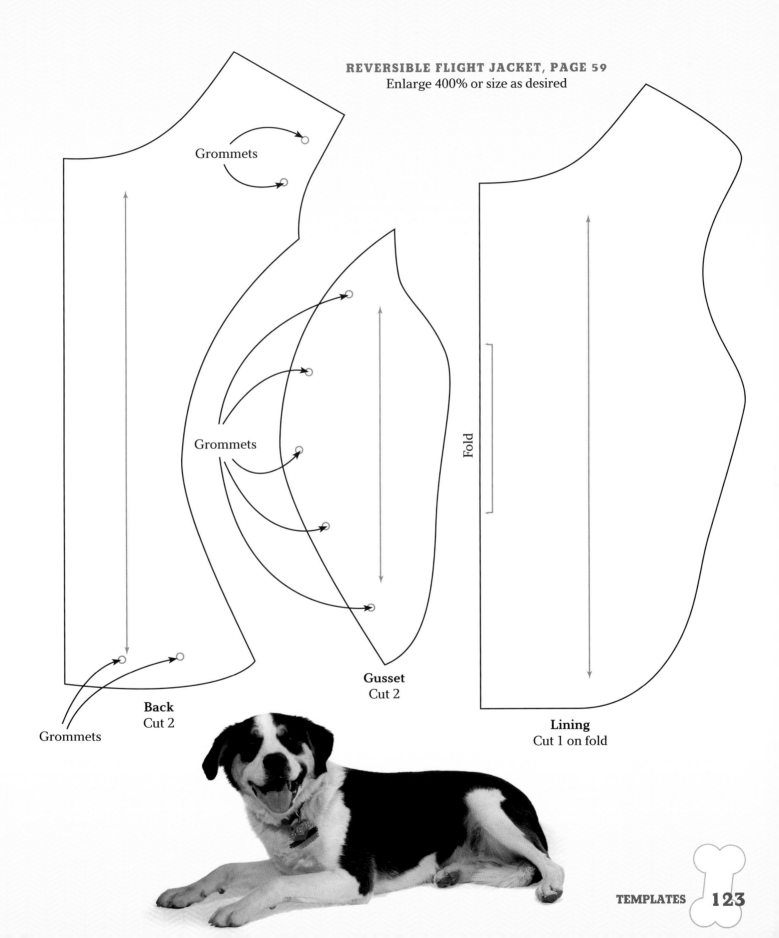

REVERSIBLE FLIGHT JACKET, PAGE 59
Enlarge 400% or size as desired

Grommets

Grommets

Grommets

Grommets

Fold

Gusset
Cut 2

Back
Cut 2

Lining
Cut 1 on fold

**WATER-BOTTLE COLLAR,
PAGE 76**
Actual size or size as desired
Embroidery transfer

Hook-and-loop tape

Flap

Flap

SAFETY VEST, PAGE 67
Size as needed per instructions on page 67

**MAD KITTY SQUEAKER
TOY, PAGE 64**
Enlarge to 12" (30.5 cm) or
other desired length

ANARCHY RULES T-SHIRT, PAGE 54
Enlarge 200% or size as desired
Cut out and save the shaded areas

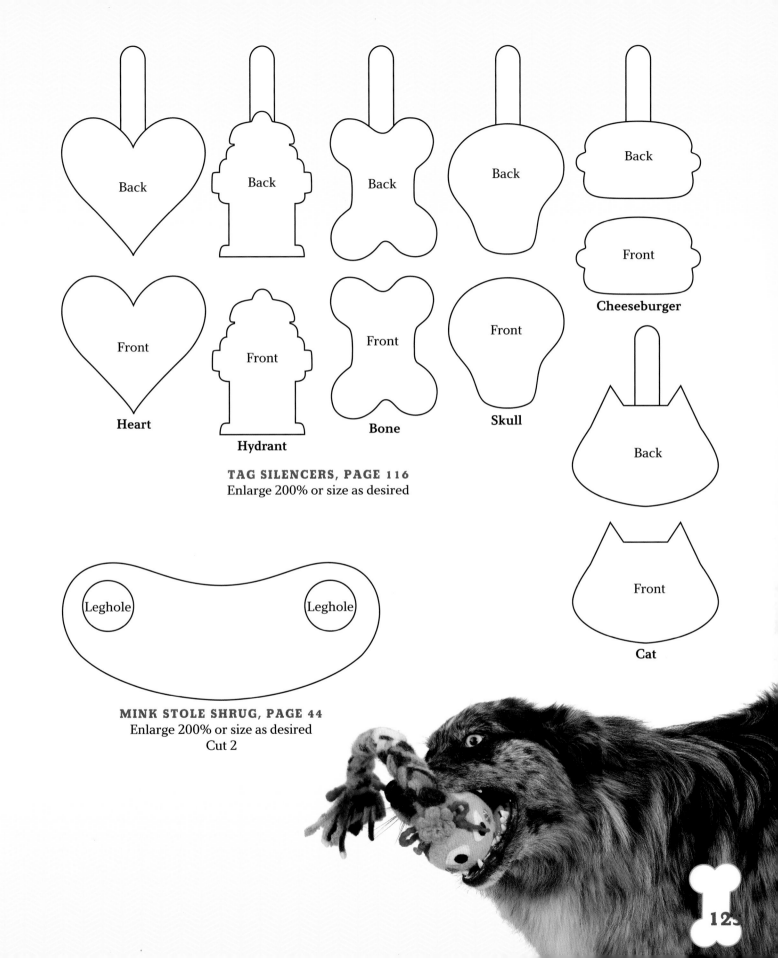

Back

Back

Back

Back

Back

Front

Front

Front

Front

Cheeseburger

Heart

Front

Hydrant

Bone

Skull

Back

Front

Cat

TAG SILENCERS, PAGE 116
Enlarge 200% or size as desired

Leghole   Leghole

MINK STOLE SHRUG, PAGE 44
Enlarge 200% or size as desired
Cut 2

About the Designers

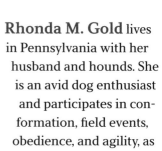

Angela Bate lives in Prince George, B.C., Canada. She has a passion for combining new and used fabrics to create beautiful things that are usable and eco-friendly. She loves to hand sew, and recently she's become addicted to embroidery. For more information, please visit her website, www.norththreads.com.

Laura Bersson lives in Charleston, South Carolina, with her boyfriend, dog, roommates, and several cats. She sewed her first doggie tee after adopting her dog, Dizzee, from the pound in January, 2006. Laura likes to spend her time baking, mixing up crazy flavors of ice cream, and crocheting hats for cats and dogs. See more at www.laurascrochet.com.

Candie Cooper specializes in creating accessible mixed media jewelry and crafts. She is the author of *Felted Jewelry* (Lark Books, 2007), which features 20 fabulous felted projects including necklaces, rings, and bracelets. Candie currently lives in Shenzhen, China. Visit Candie's website, www.candiecooper.com for a further look at her creations and a link to her online journal, The Savvy Crafter.

Rhonda M. Gold lives in Pennsylvania with her husband and hounds. She is an avid dog enthusiast and participates in conformation, field events, obedience, and agility, as well as pet-assisted therapy. Her one-of-a-kind hand-knit items incorporate hand-spun, hand-dyed fibers and 100% natural wools. Visit www.artemiswhippets.com or www.artemis1.etsy.com to learn more.

Wendi Gratz lives with her family and her sewing machine in western North Carolina. In high school she skipped home ec in favor of wood and metal shop, and didn't learn to use a sewing machine until college. Now she makes fun clothes, funky dolls, and all kinds of quilts. You can see her work at www.wendigratz.com.

Shiu Pei Luu is a 23-year-old industrial engineer, graduate art student, and a freelance illustrator living with her boyfriend in the San Francisco Bay area. Many of her pet creations and illustrations are influenced by Mimi, her one-year-old taco terrier. You can see her latest work at www.meanypie.etsy.com.

Ann Marie Matott operates Annie's Sweatshop out of her home sewing room in Athens, Georgia. Her mission is simple: to provide smart and sustainable handcrafted fashions. Nowadays you can find this Buffalo, New York, transplant soaking up the Georgia sun with her two mini-dachshunds, Porter and Stout. To find out more, visit www.anniessweatshop.com or email anniessweatshop@gmail.com.

Sue McMahon started sewing her own clothes at a very young age. After searching for an interesting collar for her dog, she took up leather crafting and has been creating unique one-of-a-kind pet collars ever since. Some of her work can be seen on Etsy.com, under her designer name: detailsbysue. She can be reached at srbphoto@hotmail.com.

Joan K. Morris's artistic endeavors have led her down many successful creative paths, including ceramics and costume design for motion pictures. Joan has contributed projects for numerous Lark books, including *Pretty Little Patchwork* (2008), *Cutting Edge Decoupage* (2007), *Creative Stitching on Paper* (2006), *Hip Handbags* (2005), and many more.

Aimee Ray has been making things for as long as she can remember. She is a graphic designer in the greeting card and comic book industries, and enjoys digital painting, illustration, sewing stuffed animals, embroidery, and everything else in between. She is the author of *Doodle Stitching* (Lark Books, 2007), a book of contemporary embroidery designs and projects. See more of Aimee's work at www.dreamfollow.com.

Amanda Rydell holds a BA in Graphic Design from the Art Institute in Minneapolis, Minnesota. After adopting Ali, her energetic Yorkie, she was overwhelmed with the high price of commercial dog clothing, and teamed up with her grandma Betty to create the Warm and Woolly Crocheted Sweater in this book. For more of their sweaters, check out www.aliandal.etsy.com.

Rachael Staples loves her dogs, and she loves to knit. It only made sense to combine her passions and to knit for her dogs Baz, a Dogue de Bordeaux, and Daisy, a Brussells Griffon. Eventually, Rachael set up Mr Soft Top luxury puppy apparel (http://www.mrsofttop.com) and has been busy ever since. She makes dog sweaters of all shapes and sizes, for the tiniest of Chihuahuas to the largest of Great Danes.

Diane Swain comes from a long line of painters, sculptors, jewelry makers, sewers, and stitchers. Diane created the colorful and comfy doggie bed in this book for her Min-Pin, Rocky. He cuddles up on it with his blanket (occasionally, under it) every night. Visit her Etsy store, www.dianerez3.etsy.com, to see her handmade dog hats, toys, and other creations.

Index

Acknowledgments

A big wag of the tail to the folks who created the projects in this book. Pups everywhere wiggle their hind ends in appreciation for these talented designers. This book wouldn't exist without them, doggonit!

Yips of gratitude to Jane LaFerla, Beth Sweet, and Kathleen McCafferty for their dogged editorial assistance.

Kristi Pfeffer earned a lick on the face for her playful art direction. Photographer Steve Mann deserves a good, long scratch on the sweet spot— you know, the place that when rubbed sets off unrestrained thumping of the leg. There are no bones to pick with associate art director Shannon Yokeley and art assistants Jeff Hamilton, Bradley Norris, and intern Meagan Shirlen; they kept the process of producing the book smoothly on track.

It was a treat to work with Adelaine Lockwood, owner of Blaze & Skyy Pet Boutique & Wellness Center in Asheville, North Carolina, who helped round up all our canine models. Finally, thanks to all the dog owners who allowed their talented pups to grace these pages.